The Inflation Myth

AND THE WONDERFUL WORLD
OF DEFLATION

By Mark Mobius

WILEY

This edition first published 2021

© 2021 Mark Mobius

Originally published in German as "Die Wahrheit über Inflation: Warum Geldentwertung jeden etwas angeht, wie sie manipuliert wird und wie man es durchschaut" © 2019 Mark Mobius

Registered office

John Wiley & Sons Ltd, The Atrium, Southern Gate, Chichester, West Sussex, PO19 8SQ, United Kingdom

For details of our global editorial offices, for customer services and for information about how to apply for permission to reuse the copyright material in this book please see our website at www.wiley.com.

Wiley publishes in a variety of print and electronic formats and by print-on-demand. Some material included with standard print versions of this book may not be included in e-books or in print-on-demand. If this book refers to media such as a CD or DVD that is not included in the version you purchased, you may download this material at http://booksupport.wiley.com. For more information about Wiley products, visit www.wiley.com.

Designations used by companies to distinguish their products are often claimed as trademarks. All brand names and product names used in this book are trade names, service marks, trademarks or registered trademarks of their respective owners. The publisher is not associated with any product or vendor mentioned in this book.

Limit of Liability/Disclaimer of Warranty: While the publisher and author have used their best efforts in preparing this book, they make no representations or warranties with respect to the accuracy or completeness of the contents of this book and specifically disclaim any implied warranties of merchantability or fitness for a particular purpose. It is sold on the understanding that the publisher is not engaged in rendering professional services and neither the publisher nor the author shall be liable for damages arising herefrom. If professional advice or other expert assistance is required, the services of a competent professional should be sought.

Library of Congress Cataloging-in-Publication Data

Names: Mobius, Mark, author.
Title: The inflation myth and the wonderful world of deflation / by Mark
   Mobius.
Description: Hoboken, NJ : Wiley, 2021. | Includes index.
Identifiers: LCCN 2020020072 (print) | LCCN 2020020073 (ebook) | ISBN
   9781119741428 (hardback) | ISBN 9781119741497 (ePDF) | ISBN
   9781119741527 (ePub)
Subjects: LCSH: Inflation (Finance) | Deflation (Finance) | Pricing.
Classification: LCC HG229 .M73 2021 (print) | LCC HG229 (ebook) | DDC
   332.4/1—dc23
LC record available at https://lccn.loc.gov/2020020072
LC ebook record available at https://lccn.loc.gov/2020020073

Cover Design: Wiley

Set in 13/17pt Adobe Garamond Pro by SPi Global, Chennai, India

Printed in Great Britain by CPI Antony Rowe

10 9 8 7 6 5 4 3 2 1

This book is dedicated to all of the people I have worked with in capital markets over the years. Many inspired me with new ideas and innovative concepts, laying the ground for me to think creatively and embark on new adventures.

CONTENTS

PREFACE

Shortly after this manuscript was handed into my publishers in early 2020, the COVID-19 outbreak shook the world and changed life as we knew it. From one day to the next, hundreds of thousands of lives were at stake and our economic systems came to a halt as governments around the world entered into unprecedented shutdowns.

In the wake of the COVID-19 crisis, we witnessed a lot of speculation about global economies slipping into recession. This, in turn, was expected to lead to a deflationary environment driven by weakening growth and demand. As a result of the crisis, we witnessed short-term price fluctuations in stock and bond markets all over the world.

However, the argument of this book is focused on the longer term trends regarding the rise and fall of economies and market.

I believe we have been putting too much weight on inflation statistics which are for a variety of reasons faulty. Despite economic slowdowns – caused by various crises over the years – advances in technology and automation are leading to continuously falling costs for goods and services. At the same time, a wave of completely new products enters the consumer stage every year, improving lives around the world. On example of how technology is reducing costs is the conference call service provided by Zoom Communications; users of their conference app dramatically increased from 10 million per day in December of 2019 to 300 million per day by April 2020. Many of these new users were using the free Zoom version, as opposed to the premium one, so paying nothing for a service that would have cost hundreds if not thousands of dollars in telephone bills just 10 or 20 years previously. To accurately depict this phenomenon of constant technological innovation in inflation statistics is at best challenging, if not impossible, as this book will show.

Another argument of this book is that the "basket" of goods and services which forms the basis of the CPI (Consumer Price Index) calculation is continuously changing, so the basket of 1900 is different from the one in 1950, and the one in 1950 is different from the one in 2000. The problem is that you are comparing different baskets of goods and services, thus rendering any comparison somewhat meaningless. Furthermore, with consumption patterns constantly changing, the basket is always a step behind when it comes to tracking "typical" spending patterns.

Over the years we have seen far-reaching changes in the way people work, shop, and spend their time. This in turn has led to significant changes in spending patterns and, in some cases, rapid price changes. Certain goods have disappeared from shelves and many services are no longer provided. So, calculations based on the "old" basket no longer reflect changes in the consumer welfare of a "typical" person, as typical consumer behavior has changed.

If inflation statistics do not accurately reflect the changes in peoples' welfare, then it does not make sense to stick to inflation targets. By 2020, central banks were learning this the hard way as their financial tools were proving less and less effective in influencing inflation numbers. What we need to recognize is the necessity of questioning the holy grail of inflation targeting and rethinking an approach that we have been following almost blindly for a long time.

This book aims to help unravel the Myth of Inflation and to provide some food for thought on the future of the inflation policies that are significantly impacting our everyday lives around the world. More importantly I want to demonstrate that, in fact, we are in a deflationary world with goods and services improving in quality and variety while declining as a percent of people's incomes.

INTRODUCTION

Inflation has been a subject for bankers, scholars, political leaders, and the general public for a long time. The rising prices of goods and services in currency terms have been condemned by people since time immemorial. There has been no let-up in everyone's desire to stop prices from rising, despite governments' continual actions to debase their currencies.

Very often governments, yielding to popular pressure, have taken draconian measures – such as prohibiting price rises and punishing those who disobeyed. In 1971, President Nixon announced a freeze on all prices and wages throughout the United States. Gerald Ford, his successor, distributed buttons with the slogan "whip inflation now." Presidential candidate Ronald Reagan announced that inflation was *as violent as a mugger, as frightening as an armed robber, and as deadly as a hit man.*

In early 2020, it seemed that the tables had turned. Central bankers and economists were worrying that inflation was disappearing and we might even have been in a deflationary era. And despite their efforts to bring inflation up, as they believed that an inflation rate of at least 2% would render economies healthy and result in economic growth, their cures did not work. Dramatic decreases in interest rates and "quantitative easing" – or money printing, with central banks buying bonds and even stocks (as in the case of Japan) to feed money into the system – failed.

But why were recognized theories not working anymore? For example, the famous Phillips Curve Theory – there is an inverse relationship between inflation and unemployment – did not seem to be valid anymore. Central bankers who promised that job growth would lead to inflation rising were proved wrong. The good news was that central bankers like Mario Draghi, the former head of the European Central Bank, and Mark Carney, governor of the Bank of England, warned that the economic policy consensus was no longer tenable. Jerome Powell, head of the US Federal Reserve, said that inflation was one of the *"major challenges of our time"*. . . and he was not referring to *too high* inflation but to *too low*. Times had really changed.

The question central banks and governments were asking themselves was what they could do to boost inflation when neither lowering interest rates (by 2020 rates in the major economies were either below 1% or, as in the case of Europe and Japan, negative) nor measures aimed at pumping liquidity into the economies were working.

One of the main reasons behind these shifts in economic practice and theory has been the acceleration of technological progress. It is driving productivity, which in turn lowers the costs of goods and services even as governments devalue their currencies by printing more and more money. Probably the best example of this technology change is Amazon and similar online shopping firms who have pushed retail costs down and decimated many parts of the traditional "offline" retail scene. Studies showed that online prices were falling steadily from 2012 and were lower than they have been at the turn of the millennium. The so-called "Amazon Effect" was not limited to Amazon. We witnessed the phenomenon in transport (Uber), hotels (trivago.com), and travel (opodo.com). But the decline in prices could be attributed not only to those organizations directly serving the public at the retail level, but also to the producer level – where improvements in automation, workflow programming, and many other innovations were pushing the costs of production down. The invention of cell phones was just the start of the crash in communication prices. Those costs continued their downward trend with the invention of internet calling and faster, cheaper smartphones.

Of course, the hapless gatherers of inflation statistics have been in a quandary because of the avalanche of new, innovative, or significantly improved products as a result of technological innovation. This has made the task of measuring inflation an impossible one. A study by economists Austan D. Goolsbee and Peter J. Klenow found that even excluding clothing, 44% of online sales in an Adobe Analytics database were of goods that **did not exist the year before!** The net entry of new goods alone led to the CPI overstating true inflation by 1.5 to 2.5 percentage points per year. They also found that online prices for bedding and furniture fell by about 12% between January 2014 to June 2019 but the official consumer price index fell by only 2.1%.[1]

More importantly, the proliferation of free services throws any effort to measure inflation completely out of whack. I now can make a video call anywhere in the world, obtain information on any subject, and translate languages free of charge. Ten years ago, or even five years ago, would it have been free? And how much would those services have cost? Erik Brynjolfsson and his research team at MIT tried to measure the value to users of various free online services by withholding those services from respondents temporarily and asking them how much they would pay to get them back. Questioning several respondents, they found that, for example, the value of not giving up WhatsApp was worth about $600 to the respondents. To give up free online search engines for a year, people on average responded that they would want to be paid over $17,000.

---

[1]http://www.klenow.com/internet-rising-prices-falling_Goolsbee_Klenow.pdf.

David Byrne of the Federal Reserve and Carol Corrado of the Conference Board constructed a digital access services index that showed prices for internet services falling by 21% between 2007 and 2017 while the official price index for internet access showed prices rising by 4.5%.

Another factor in the deflation phenomenon is the spread of global trade. Despite the trade war between the US and China, the fact remains that world trade is on the rise – with a pause in 2020 as a result of the COVID-19 crisis. According to the World Bank trade grew from 39% as a share of the world GDP to 59% between 1990 and 2018. This explosion of trade resulted in global competition for lower production and distribution costs as well as a rapid rise in information exchange which spurred innovation and change. The spread of deflation covers the globe. When American oil men discovered a way to extract oil and gas from rock using innovative fracking methods, oil prices globally were driven down – even when their methods initially were more expensive than the production costs in Saudi Arabia.

In this book I want to lay out the following ideas.

Firstly, inflation statistics are of immense interest to governments around the world because rising prices elicit a political response among their constituents. Governments often rise and fall on the perception people have about the prices of goods and services they consume.

Therefore, governments try their best to measure inflation. In doing so, they simplify, generalize, and – in some
cases – falsify or try to control the numbers by taking
many actions, such as placing price controls on various
products and services, so people are not aware of the
actual price changes – leading to a black market and
shortages.

  Secondly, the measurement of inflation is severely
flawed; not because the diligent people who gather statistics regarding the prices of goods and services around the
world are unqualified or unfaithful to their trade, but
because they are not only shooting at a moving target –
with prices changing up or down on a minute by minute
basis – but also the very nature of the products and
services they are trying to measure is continuously changing. The desire for simplification in constructing an index
that will encompass the multitude of prices, and reflect
the buying habits of the entire population, is a thankless
task and one doomed to severe imperfections.

  **Thirdly, currencies, the measuring stick used to
monitor price changes, have throughout history been
debased by every authority that issued them.** Many
forms of currency have been tried: gold coins, silver coins,
tin coins, copper coins, seashells, paper bills, and others
have all fallen by the wayside as a result of debasement.
Currencies are created by human beings, and thus can be
degraded or upgraded by them to be worth more or less
than the market believes. Thus, a unit of currency one

day will be different in the eyes of the buyer or seller on another day. On that note: Throughout this book we use the word "inflation" but each time the word is used "currency devaluation" should replace it. So-called "inflation" is really the loss in purchasing value of a currency.

Fourthly, advances in technology and automation are leading to continuously falling costs for many goods and services. At the same time, every year a multitude of completely new and innovative products enter the consumer stage and improve people's lives around the world.

Finally, incomes in currency terms or the buying power of consumers change continuously, and, in fact, for most of history, they have tended to match price increases. Therefore, although it may seem that inflation is taking place for some products and services, they are actually getting cheaper in terms of the earning power of the consumer.

If you take all of the above together I am sure you will agree with me that our understanding of inflation is to say the least flawed. I would even go a step further: In my opinion the concept of inflation is a myth, a legend, a fable, and, yes, a falsehood for a number of reasons. What we are experiencing today is, in fact, a deflationary spiral driven by innovation and automation. This deflationary phenomenon is here to stay and will continue to improve our standard of living. Welcome to the wonderful world of deflation!

ACKNOWLEDGMENTS

Special thanks to Anna von Hahn who gave invaluable help in editing this book and helping me to clarify many points. I would also like to thank my publisher, especially Gladys Ganaden for taking such excellent care of *The Inflation Myth* during the publication process. My books have always been in the best possible hands at Wiley. Last but not least, appreciation to Kelly Falconer for her great performance as my agent and also to Graeme Falconer for his support.

ABOUT THE AUTHOR

Mark Mobius is a founding partner of Mobius Capital Partners. Previously he was executive chairman of the Templeton Emerging Markets Group and spent over 30 years investing in emerging markets all over the world. He received a PhD from the Massachusetts Institute of Technology. Mark is on the International Finance Corporation's Economic Advisory Board and served on the World Bank's Global Corporate Governance Forum as co-chairman of its Investor Responsibility Task Force. Mark is the author of several books including: *Invest for Good* (2019); *The Little Book of Emerging Markets* (2012); *Passport to Profits* (1999/2012); *Mobius on Emerging Markets* (1996); *The Investor's Guide to Emerging Markets* (1994); *Equities, An Introduction to Core Concepts* (2006); *Bonds, An Introduction to Core Concepts* (2012); *and Mutual Funds, An Introduction to Core Concepts* (2007).

www.markmobius.com

1 History and Inflation

My interest in inflation was piqued when in 2007 Argentina's director of consumer pricing, Graciela Bevacqua, at the INDEC, the official statistics agency, was fired for not being willing to falsify her agency's inflation statistics to satisfy the government led by President Cristina Fernández de Kirchner. The situation became a global incident when the International Monetary Fund (IMF) gave a report on Argentina to the IMF board which could have resulted in the country being censured and expelled from the IMF. The official Argentine data reported inflation at 10%, while independent data provided by as many as nine private agencies indicated that inflation was actually more than double that at between 25% and 30%. The government's efforts to keep the numbers low and fool the public were in response to rising prices that had resulted in mass protests against the Kirchner government. When IMF Chair Christine Lagarde said that if Argentina did not start producing reliable statistics, she would give the country a "red card," Kirchner – speaking at the UN General Assembly – said: *"Argentina is not a soccer team, it's a sovereign country and accepts no threats or pressures. . . In the game of comparing football with economics and politics, let me say that the President of FIFA has been far more successful and satisfactory than that of the IMF Executive Board."*[1] (Of course, that was before the FIFA Board was found to be engaged in rampant corruption.) In 2007, the Kirchner government not only dismissed Graciela Bevacqua, but also fined her and charged her with embezzlement. Graciela spoke out and claimed that her superiors had asked her to delete decimals from the inflation calculations. The American Statistical Association protested the persecution its colleague was facing in Argentina, but to no avail. Graciela was replaced. More of that case later.

History as Inflation

"I do not think it an exaggeration," the economist Friedrich Hayek once wrote, *"to say that history is largely a history of inflation. . ."*[2] Price rises can be witnessed

around the world, as indicated by Germany's Weimar Republic hyperinflation in the early 1920s, the inflation of Eastern Europe following the collapse of the Berlin Wall in 1989, the stagflation of many Western countries in the 1970s, and the inflation that Japan witnessed following the end of the economic miracle in the 1960s.

It's important for us to look at the consequences of such information flows regarding "inflation," "deflation," "hyperinflation," etc. and what are the effects on decision-making not only in governments but also in business and investment. We want to look at the impact of inflation/deflation statistical information flows and how they can be so misleading.

Importance of Inflation Numbers

Ever since the earliest price indices were first introduced at the start of the eighteenth century, the measurement of inflation and attempts to control its growth have become increasingly salient. After the Second World War, full employment was seen as one of the major goals of economic policy. Then, over the next forty years, price stability took its place as the primary economic aim of governments and central banks. As mentioned previously, it was Ronald Reagan in the

1980s who described the threat of inflation as being "*. . .as violent as a mugger, as frightening as an armed robber and as deadly as a hitman.*"[3] Showing the priorities of modern governments, in 1991 the then British Chancellor, Norman Lamont, told the House of Commons that: "*. . . rising unemployment and the recession have been the price that we have had to pay to get inflation down. That price is well worth paying. That focus on keeping inflation down remains at the heart of monetary policy.*"[4]

Central banks around the world are charged with keeping inflation at an agreed rate. For example, in the UK each year, the Chancellor of the Exchequer writes to the Governor of the Bank, confirming what the inflation target is. Should the inflation rate deviate from this target by more than 1%, the Governor must write to the Chancellor, explaining why the inflation target has been missed and what steps the Bank is going to take to rectify the situation.

Price instability is, of course, not just an issue for governments. For investors, information regarding the rate of inflation plays an important part in deciding where they put their money. Rising levels of inflation supposedly reduce the value of savings and investment unless interest rates and returns on investment keep pace. This has an impact on everyone – from those with savings in a bank account, to where pension funds are being invested.

The Long Coffin

At the center of the Bank of England is a small courtyard garden, which is the preserve of the incumbent governor. Originally, the garden was a graveyard. When the Bank moved to Threadneedle Street in 1734, it soon expanded to take over the church next door which was subsequently deconsecrated and demolished. However, the decision was taken to leave the graveyard there. In the 1920s and 1930s, when the Bank needed rebuilding again, the Garden Court was dug up to reveal several coffins, one of which was the curiosity of William Jenkins. Jenkins worked at the Bank in the late 1700s, was 6 feet 7 inches tall, and was buried in the Garden Court as his friends were worried that his body might be stolen and sold. Such was the size of Jenkins' coffin that when it was moved to Nunhead Cemetery, it had to be placed in the catacombs as it was too long for the vaults.

Back at the restored Garden Court meanwhile, as part of the renovations the Court was planted with mulberry trees. The reason for the choice of trees was twofold. First, there was the practical consideration that the roots of the mulberry tree grow horizontally, rather than straight down into the ground: handy when the Bank of England's gold vaults (which contain some 400,000 bars of gold) are directly underneath. Second, and more symbolically, the mulberry tree has played a critical role in the history of money. In seventh-century

China, the bark of the mulberry tree was used to make the earliest form of paper currency. The old saying has it that money doesn't grow on trees. But in early China, it did; and when it arrived, inflation was swift to follow.

Marco Polo and Money

In 1271, the traveler and explorer Marco Polo set off for the court of Khubilai (otherwise known as Kublai Khan) the same year the latter established the Yuan Dynasty and became Emperor of China. Polo's journey to reach Khubilai's court at Shangdu took him four years and was not without incident: the fall of the city of Xiangyang in 1273 to Khubilai's troops was just one episode in which Polo was involved. All of this, and his impressions of Khubilai's court, Polo wrote up in a book that in France was traditionally called *Le Livre des Merveilles (The Book of Marvels)* and which is known in English more prosaically as, simply, *The Travels*.

Out of the many marvels that Marco Polo was struck by was the Yuan Dynasty's use of banknotes. *"The emperor's mint is in this city of Khanbaliq,"* he wrote, *"and it is set up in such a way that might well say he has mastered the art of alchemy."* Polo described in detail how the Great Khan, as he called him, went about making the notes: *"He has the bark stripped from trees – to be precise, from the mulberry trees whose leaves are eaten by silkworms. Then the thin layer of bast fiber between the bark and the wood of the tree is removed. After being ground and pounded it is pressed with the aid of glue into sheets like those of cotton paper, which are completely black. And when these sheets are ready, they are cut up into pieces of different sizes, rectangular in shape and of greater length than breadth. And they are made with such authority and solemnity as if they were cast from pure gold or silver . . . when everything has been done correctly the chief of the officials deputed by the emperor dips the seal entrusted to him in cinnabar and stamps it on the piece of money, so that the imprint of the seal dipped in the cinnabar remains impressed upon it; and then the money is legal tender.*"[5]

Polo's enthusiasm for paper money is proof of how far ahead China was in its understanding of monetary policy in comparison to their Western counterparts: it wasn't until the seventeenth century that paper bills began to be used in Europe. But what Marco Polo had been so impressed by, wasn't something new to China. In fact, the concept had its origins several hundred years earlier during the Tang Dynasty of 618–907. Here, bills of exchange, printed on pieces of textile, were used by businessmen and government officials to take money from one city to another. The notes were known as Feiqian or "flying money," on account of the money being able to "fly" back without the need for coins or gold.

But it was not long after the invention of the idea that the appearance of inflation followed suit. An official version of Jiaozi, or certificate of exchange, was launched in 1023, with the stipulation that the notes were convertible to coins. However, the pressure on government finances due to fighting wars resulted in the printing of more Jiaozi. By devaluing the notes against the coins they were meant to represent, the result was a sharp rise in inflation – by 1107, there was 20 times the total amount of Jiaozi compared to the initial launch. The result was that the notes were ultimately withdrawn and replaced with a new set of notes: to avoid another round of rising prices, a set percentage of the printing of any new notes had to be matched by an increase in coin reserves.

By the 1160s, the now dominant Southern Song Dynasty added a further stipulation – all notes were to be recalled and redeemed for copper coins every three years. This was a system that held until, once again, the need to finance military activity saw a relaxing of these rules and the printing of paper notes rose again. By the time of Marco Polo's travels, the now dominant Yuan Dynasty had issued national paper currency, with which it guaranteed convertibility into silver, and banned the use of coins in trading, forcing the use of the new currency.

Gold and Silver Coins

For a while, and during Marco Polo's visit, the system worked. But as the Mongolian Empire expanded, the monetary rules were not always followed through – gold and silver coins ended up being used in some places again. As with previous dynasties, the printing of additional notes to fund military activity was a harbinger of the end of the regime. The Yuan Dynasty's successor, the Ming Dynasty, began its reign in 1368 and would rule China for the next 277 years until the mid-seventeenth century. To begin with, the new regime under Emperor Chu Yuan-chang returned the money supply to coinage: in 1361, prior to his rise to Emperor, he ordered the making of a new mint of copper coins. Coins then became the sole currency until 1375, when lack of sufficient copper supplies saw a return to paper currency. However, the circulation of coins continued until the end of the century, and it was only via the third Ming emperor, Yung-lo, that coins were successfully removed from circulation – a decision, perhaps unsurprisingly given previous Chinese rulers, that was the result of the need to fund military campaigns.

Both under Chu Yuan-chang and Yung-lo, the use of paper currency was marked by a sustained rise in prices. As described in *Hyperinflation: A World History* by He Liping, rice prices rose 6.6% annually for this 50-year period and under Yung-lo's rule, when paper currency was in sole use, it rose 11% annually. As well as rice, there were also large rises in the price of gold, silver, copper, and grain. The result was that by 1435, the paper currency was dropped altogether. Copper coins were minted again, as they would be for the remainder of the Ming Dynasty: silver, too, grew in circulation, with the government allowing people to pay their land tax in silver. Trade with the rest of the world also grew and this, too, was paid in silver.

Not only did the Ming Dynasty not return to paper currency, its successor – the Qing Dynasty – also eschewed the paper system for almost all of its 200-plus years rule. The two exceptions to this were between 1651 and 1661, and between 1853 and 1861, both to fund military activity. In the latter case, Emperor Hsien-Feng attempted to overcome previous problems by setting up a system of Coin Houses. The idea was that people with paper currency could exchange them for silver notes, which in turn could be exchanged for silver or copper coins. This convertibility, in theory, should have set the value of the notes and enforced people's faith in them. In practice, the Coin Houses didn't offer the full value of coins or silver notes but demanded substantial discounts in order to exchange them.

Today, the Ming banknote is a historical artifact, with an example on display at the British Museum, which was featured in the BBC series *A History of the World in 100 Objects*. The British Museum note is worth 1,000 coins, with the design showing a drawing of the number of coins it represents. In practical terms, it was clearly a great step forward: this one note was the equivalent of 3 kilograms or 1.5 meters of copper coins (Chinese coins at the time had a hole in the center so they could be collected onto a piece of string – a long piece of string in this case!). That was the theory, anyway. Fifteen years after the launch of the paper currency, this 1,000-cash note was worth just 250 coins. And while a note from the time of the currency claimed, "Whenever paper money is presented, copper coins will be paid out, and whenever paper money is issued, copper coins will be paid in," the governmental urge to print more money rendered it unworkable. While the note bears the legend "to circulate forever" it is today instead a historic reminder of another system that went wrong.

Money and Trust

Interviewed for a BBC series, the former Governor of the Bank of England, Mervyn King, said: "Money was invented in order to get around the problems of trusting other individuals. But then the question is, could you trust the person who issued the money?" Pressed on whether paper currency was always a flawed system by nature, King was curiously circumspect: "If you'd asked me four, five years ago, before the financial crisis, I would have said no. I think we've now worked out how to manage paper money." Perhaps in the light of the financial crisis, we should be a bit more cautious, and maybe, to quote Zhou Enlai, another great Chinese figure who when asked about the impact of the French Revolution supposedly said: *", it's too soon to tell."*

Maybe we should say about paper money, after 700 years, that it is perhaps too soon to tell. The point about paper money and inflation is, in fact, a wider one: namely that, over time, no currency keeps its value. This is a fact reinforced by the inability of governments of all stripes to resist the temptation to expand the money supply when the need (or in some cases, the greed) arises. I've used China as an example here because paper money was developed there first, but the same situation can be seen in any economy.

For many years Franz Pick, an Austrian School economist, studied currencies around the world. I remember receiving his annual currency yearbook which had information regarding all the world's currencies. He continued to study currencies all his life. He was the one who said: *"No currency holds its value"* and was a believer in gold as the best foundation for currency since his experience and studies showed that without a specific commodity base, such as gold, governments would always devalue their currencies.

The Urge to Debase

Governments' urge to increase the money supply pre-
dates the invention of paper money. The idea of coinage
is sometimes dated back to the eighth century BC, and
their use in Lydia in Asia Minor (modern Turkey). Here,
a combination of abundant gold and developments in
metallurgy combined to create a system of standardized
gold coins. Over the following centuries, the practicali-
ties of using coins in comparison to bullion saw its use
spread. But as coinage came into common usage, it
wasn't long before governments sought different ways of
manipulating the currency for their own gain. Rather
than the purity of the earliest gold and silver coins,
governments would order the reduction of the value of
precious metals, debasing them with other metals or
reducing their weight.

In the fourth century BC, Dionysius, the tyrant of
Syracuse, who ruled a Greek colony on Sicily, had the
brainwave of dealing with rising debts by changing the
face of all the local Drachmae. Ordering all coins to be
handed in, he restamped each single Drachmae to be
worth two (and thus halved his debt at a stroke). He then
went on to issue a further set of tin coins, insisting these
were valued the same as the silver Drachmae.

Dionysius' actions are the earliest, or at least one of
the earliest, examples of a ruler increasing the money
supply for their own ends. Back in China, Wang Mang's
short reign as the thirteenth Emperor of the Western

Han Dynasty (or the founder of the Xin Dynasty, depending on which historical view you take) was dominated by his economic reforms.

Wang Mang became Emperor in AD 9, but had been acting Emperor for two years before this – the emperor proper, Emperor Ping, was a young child. Wang Mang took advantage to take over as emperor himself. Wang Mang's reign was short (he died in AD 23) but he immediately set about enacting some serious monetary reforms. In the early years of his reign, he nationalized gold and ordered people to hand it in, in return for his new coinage. All private coinage was banned with prison sentences for those who used it. Later on, even those who knew people were using other coinage but didn't report it were imprisoned (as many as 100,000 people were imprisoned under these rules).

As for Wang Mang's own currency, these new coins were markedly debased compared to what they were replacing: in terms of gold, they were worth almost half as much. Added to this, the number of different coins in Wang Mang's scheme was bafflingly complex: there were 28 denominations of coins in total. According to He Liping's account, these actions were less to do with reducing debt than about shoring up Wang Mang's political position at the expense of wealthy nobles. While he might have had some success there, inflation soon followed, as much as can be deduced from the surviving documents of the time: the price of rice rose four times in a year, for example. And despite Wang Mang's best efforts, his subjects stopped using the official currency, instead returning to gold and the coins of the previous regime.

Rome's Debasement

One of the most sustained programs of coin debasement took place during the Roman Empire. Following on from Augustus' original minting of Roman coins in the form of gold Aureus and silver Denarius, a succession of subsequent emperors took turns in debasing the currency until it was all but worthless. Nero began this process in the first century AD, reducing the silver content and increasing the base metal content in the coins to 10%. Later in the same century, Emperor Trajan reduced the amount of silver in the Denarius still further. The process continued until, during the reign of Antoninianus, the amount of silver in the Denarius was down to just 5%. A century later under Gallienus, the silver content was further reduced, with the Denarius containing one five-thousandth of the silver from Augustus' reign. Unable to reduce the silver content in any meaningful way still further, Gallienus' successor Aurelian increased the face value of new coins two and a half times. The result of this debasement was twofold. First, people kept hold of earlier coins, especially gold ones, as they knew the value of their replacements would decrease. Second, the Roman Empire suffered from sharp inflation. Just as Wang Mang's coin debasement had led to a rise in rice prices, so the Roman debasement saw a rise in wheat prices: rising 32 times in Egypt, for example, between the first and third century, then 44 times in the next 30 years and at an annual rate of 24% in the subsequent decade. Real wages fell, with soldiers increasingly paid in food and clothes, rather than cash. While not the only contributing factor, economic mismanagement was one of many reasons behind the inevitable collapse of the Roman Empire.

England's Debasement

Over a millennium later, the same mistakes were being made again, this time by Henry VIII, King of England between 1509 and 1547. In the latter part of his reign, financial problems led to the decision to debase the currency. The process began in Ireland in 1536, with silver coins minted with 90% of precious metal in comparison to earlier coins. This first debasement having passed relatively unnoticed, Henry and his successors tried the trick again – six times in total under Henry, six under his successor Edward VI, then two further mintings under Mary I and Elizabeth I, respectively. Between

1544 and 1551, under Henry and Edward, the process was the most advanced and became known as the Great Debasement. By the end of the process, the value of a silver coin had been reduced to just a quarter of its previous worth. Inflation, of course, continued to grow: in the 1530s and 1540s, it grew by about 29% in comparison to the 20 years before; in the two decades that followed, it grew to 91%. Once again, there is evidence of people holding on to their earlier non-debased coins, as they knew they were of better value.

Shells and Money

Just as the Bank of England has the symbolic mulberry trees in its Garden Court, so the Museum of the National Bank of Belgium has its own artifact from the history of money: cowrie shells. The cowrie is, in fact, a sea snail which lives in the warm waters of the Indian and Pacific Oceans. Its shell is small, egg-shaped, and relatively uniform in size and nature. Before paper money, before coins, it was the cowrie shell that was used as a form of early currency in China. In the late 1970s, during an excavation of the ancient ruins of Yin, the capital of the Shang civilization, which existed from 1766–1045 BC, archaeologist Zheng Zhenxiang uncovered the tomb of Fu Hao, a female general. The tomb was one of the most important finds in Chinese

archaeology. The tomb consisted of a 20-meter wooden
chamber, the coffin of Fu Hao, and 16 human sacrifices.
As well as this, the grave revealed hundreds of ceremonial
bronze vessels, jades, and bone carvings, and more than
7,000 cowrie shells. The tomb of Fu Hao was not the
only evidence that cowrie shells were used as currency.
An inscription found on a bronze wine vessel from the
following Zhou Dynasty included an inscription of how
the maker was paid for producing this unique artifact: *"I
was given thirty strings of cowrie shells, and with this, I
made for the Duke this precious vessel."* As well as this, the
Chinese symbol for money from the Shang era is a
pictographic representation of a shell. This "radical" – a
rectangle with two internal horizontal lines and two
feet – can be found today as the root for numerous
Chinese words regarding money, including treasure,
collateral, wealth, buy, and sell.

Although a seemingly primitive form of currency, in
many respects cowrie shells were an extremely effective
unit of trade. They were portable, non-perishable, and
regular in size. And unlike their successors in the form of
coins and paper money, they weren't easily manipulated
by those in charge: you couldn't debase a shell or print
more when the financial going got rough. The shells
found in the Shang tombs near Anyang came from thes
Indian Ocean – a huge distance for the time. In the
nearby basin of the Yellow River, cowrie shells were

all but impossible to find. What this meant, basically, was that unlike the subsequent use of coins and paper money, the money supply was essentially fixed. The cowrie shells held their value as a unit of wealth.

The Shang civilization wasn't the only one to use shells as a form of currency: shell money was used in West Africa up until the mid-nineteenth century. They were used in Orissa, India, until the British East India Company replaced them at the start of the nineteenth century. On the American Pacific coast, Native Americans used them. And on the South Pacific Islands, small shells were ground down to a required size to create shell bead currency. In early China, their use as a system eventually broke down as the size of the economy grew: there weren't enough shells to keep up with the pace of growth. Later, Shang graves revealed the existence of bronze pieces in the shape of cowries to replicate cowrie shells; in effect, becoming one of the world's first minted coinages.

Summary

As we can see, the history of inflation is closely linked with a history of debasement. And there we encounter a first problem when measuring inflation: If currencies are continually being debased by the governments who issue them how can we measure inflation in currency terms? Is it possible to create a form of money where the supply is

fixed, and thus is able to hold its value? Can a currency
be created that is beyond the whims of government needs
and that people can trust absolutely as a source of wealth?
One possible attempt to answer this question is via the
creation of so-called cryptocurrencies and, in particular,
that of Bitcoin. But even with these instruments, the
ability to produce new supply through the production
of complex calculations, or other opaque operations,
renders these new instruments highly suspect. The wild
fluctuations of the cryptocurrencies in sovereign currency
terms give a hint of their instability.

2 The Critical Importance of Inflation Numbers

Inflation statistics are one of the most important statistics used by governments and businesses around the world. They provide a benchmark to determine wage settlements, railroad fares, water bills, pensions, and many other items touching the lives of millions of people. In fact, we might say that central banks almost worship the inflation numbers that they receive, so that when the numbers rise, banks have a reason to raise interest rates in the belief that by doing so they will reduce inflation. You could say that inflation numbers have almost tyrannical power!

Making Important Policy Decisions on Inflation Data

In 2008, during the height of the subprime crisis in the US, when it looked like the US financial system could collapse, the Federal Reserve decided not to lower interest rates even as the economy looked to be on the verge of depression. But the Fed was concerned about inflation and in a statement said: *"... the downside risks to growth and the upside risks to inflation are both of significant concern to the Committee."*[6] Later in his memoir, former Chairman Bernanke wrote that *"... in retrospect, that decision was certainly a mistake."*[7]

International Interest in Inflation

There is global interest in measuring inflation. According to the IMF, there are 181 countries that have an inflation index, specifically the CPI (Consumer Price Index). Countries with inflation statistics are found on all continents. Of course, all the developed countries have CPIs, but a long list of developing and very small countries are included in the list. Even San Marino, that microstate in north-central Italy, is included. I suppose polling the consumption behavior of the 30,000 San Marino population must be an easy process!

One interesting case is China, which, though one country, has three separate entries on the list: "China P.R. Hong Kong"; "China P.R. Macao"; and "China P.R. Mainland."

Countries With Inflation Statistics

Afghanistan, Albania, Algeria, Angola, Anguilla, Antigua, Argentina, Armenia, Aruba, Australia, Austria, Bahamas, Bahrain, Bangladesh, Barbados, Belgium, Belize, Benin, Bhutan, Bolivia, Bosnia and Herzegovina, Botswana, Brazil, Brunei, Bulgaria, Burkina Faso, Burundi, Cambodia, Cameroon, Canada, Cape Verde, Central African Republic, Chad, Chile, China P.R. Mainland, China P.R. Macao, China P.R. Hong Kong, Colombia, Comoros, Congo, Costa Rica, Cote d'Ivoire, Croatia, Curacao, Cyprus, Czech Republic, Denmark, Djibouti, Dominica, Dominican Republic, Ecuador, Egypt, El Salvador, Equatorial Guinea, Estonia, Ethiopia, Fiji, Finland, France, Gabon, Gambia, Georgia, Germany, Ghana, Greece, Grenada, Guatemala, Guinea, Guinea-Bissau, Guyana, Haiti, Honduras, Hungary, Iceland, India, Indonesia, Iran, Iraq, Ireland, Israel, Italy, Jamaica, Japan, Jordan, Kazakhstan, Kenya, Korea, Kosovo,

Kuwait, Kyrgyz, Laos, Latvia, Lebanon, Lesotho, Lithuania, Luxembourg, Macedonia, Madagascar, Malawi, Malaysia, Maldives, Mali, Malta, Mauritania, Mauritius, Mexico, Moldova, Mongolia, Montenegro, Montserrat, Morocco, Mozambique, Myanmar, Namibia, Nepal, Netherlands, Netherlands Antilles, New Zealand, Nicaragua, Niger, Nigeria, Norway, Oman, Pakistan, Panama, Papua New Guinea, Paraguay, Peru, Philippines, Poland, Portugal, Qatar, Romania, Russian Federation, Rwanda, Samoa, San Marino, Sao Tome and Principe, Saudi Arabia, Senegal, Republic of Serbia, Seychelles, Sierra Leone, Singapore, Sint Maarten, Slovak Republic, Slovenia, Solomon Islands, South Africa, South Sudan, Spain, Sri Lanka, St. Kitts and Nevis, St. Lucia, St. Vincent and the Grenadines, Sudan, Suriname, Swaziland, Sweden, Switzerland, Tanzania, Thailand, Democratic Republic of Timor-Leste, Togo, Tonga, Trinidad and Tobago, Tunisia, Turkey, Uganda, Ukraine, United Arab Emirates, United Kingdom, United States, Uruguay, Vanuatu, Venezuela, Vietnam, West Bank and Gaza, Republic of Yemen, Zambia, Zimbabwe

The Influential Measure

In an article in the August 24, 2016 issue of *The Times,* economics editor Philip Aldrick said it was hard to think of a more influential economic measure than inflation, since it was the benchmark against which wage settlements were struck, to which rail fares were determined, and water bills fixed. Baby boomers and public sector pensioners tracked it and benefit claimants depended on it. It had the power to cripple incomes, and central banks were in thrall to it for determining their policies regarding interest rates. He said there was a kind of tyranny of inflation that boiled down to a handful of numbers. He added that for a measure that was so significant, one would think that it would be subject to very high-quality testing, but that was not the case. In the UK, the consumer index which was so widely followed had been until May 2016 compiled under European regulations dating from 1995 and last meaningfully modified six years previously. Consumer prices were supposed to be a proxy for the cost of living, but the chief economist of the Bank of England said that this was not the best measure because it excluded housing costs. The Office for National Statistics agreed that the Consumer Price Index (CPI) was not a cost-of-living index since it excluded housing which is a large part of most people's living expenses. Aldrick wrote that the CPI ignored the fact that people tended to substitute for cheaper items and the rise of discounters, such as the retail discounters Aldi and Lidl, resulted in changing spending habits.

Data gathering methods in the UK were antiquated, Aldrick wrote. Contractors collected 110,000 prices every month from 140 stores and also added another 70,000 prices from catalogs and websites. He suggested instead that retailers scanning data and checkouts would provide a more accurate picture of spending behavior. Also, studying websites where a fifth of non-food purchases was made in the UK would be more accurate. Of course, changes are being made and data-gathering upgraded, but keeping up with changing circumstances is certainly challenging.

Impact on Individual Lives

In America during the 1960s and 1970s, before they depended on inflation indices, the US government raised Social Security benefits by simply making a judgment from time to time as to what they thought price rises were in order to offset the effects of inflation on the purchasing power of Social Security beneficiaries. Indexing started in 1975 in the belief that formal indexing provided a reliable method to offset the effects of inflation, since it was believed that legislation tended to increase benefits more than what was justified by real inflation as politicians were pressured to be more generous to recipients (who were also voters). It was learned that the indexing tended to overstate inflation, but there was political reluctance to downgrade payments since the bias was judged to be small. Of course, it was easy to overlook the fact that even a 1% error, which in the moment seemed small, could result in a much bigger error over time as a result of compounding.

The Popularity of Inflation Numbers

On almost a daily basis, you can pick up a newspaper or log onto the internet and find some critical reference to inflation as regards to government policy. One headline warned that the Federal Reserve should wake up and admit that the US was overheating – as indicated by rising inflation numbers. The article referred to how consumer prices had risen to 2.3% year-on-year and that by excluding the so-called volatile food and categories, the "core" personal consumption expenditures inflation number had moved to 2%, matching the government's inflation target. The article then went on to say that the recent increase in the federal fund's rate to a range of 1.75 to 2% meant that the Fed had finally brought real (nominal rates minus inflation) interest rates to about zero. A continuation of that situation neither stimulated nor slowed economic activity, it said. The assumption was made that there was a direct link between the economy's growth, inflation, and interest rates; an assumption that has been questioned by some but embraced by many.

India Stops Futures Trading To Influence Inflation

In 2008, the Indian government suspended futures trading for some commodities in order to control inflation. The government judged that the futures markets contributed to India's rise in food prices. For a government facing an election, the desire was to downplay inflation numbers. There was a danger that news of higher inflation would result in the incumbent government losing the election. By introducing a series of distortions in the market – such as banning futures trading in some commodities, banning the exports of milk powder, and continuing to subsidize fuel prices before the election – the government was trying to influence what was actually happening to the inflation numbers. The response to inflation numbers also caused the policymakers in India to influence the currency exchange rate. It was estimated that a 1% appreciation in the Rupee yielded a 0.2% reduction in the wholesale price index. Therefore, the government attempted to pursue a strong rupee policy by taking a number of measures with regards to the country's foreign reserves.

China's Efforts To Influence The CPI Numbers

In 2011, China's central bank, the People's Bank of China, raised one-year borrowing and lending rates by 0.25% in an effort to influence what they thought was increasing inflation. China's CPI, the main gauge of inflation for the policymakers, was rising but the changes did not seem to be statistically significant. For example, during the whole of 2010, the CPI was up 3.3%, exceeding the government's target to keep it below 3%; but some asked if the difference was that significant. In that same year, the government, based on their belief that inflation was on the rise, raised the reserve requirements for banks and told them to reduce their lending.

The Effect of Mexican Tomatoes On Inflation

In 1987, the Mexican government introduced a new emergency anti-inflation program when inflation rates showed a large increase. The program promised to be unpopular and even President Miguel de la Madrid said that it included "strong measures, bitter measures, painful measures." The inflation numbers showed a 150% increase. As the labor unions were pressing for a 46% increase in the minimum wage, the government announced a 38% rise in the minimum wage while also announcing rises in gasoline and electric power prices. Clearly, what the unions and the government were proposing was out of sync with what the inflation numbers indicated. One official was quoted as saying that, in theory, their program could get the inflation down, but it was hard to convey to the public how inflation could be decreased by increasing the price of gasoline and electricity! Then, at the end of that year, the Mexican government announced a new basket of 75 consumer goods and services to be used to gauge wage increases. This move dispensed with the old system of using the inflation rate set by the country's central bank, which some considered a bad joke since it fell so short of the actual price of goods being sold in shops.

Illustrating how one product price can influence thoughts about inflation is the example of tomato prices in Mexico. In 2000, a sharp rise in tomato prices, an important part of Mexican households' diet, pushed inflation well above expectations. The weight of tomatoes in the Mexican inflation index was high as they are used in a wide variety of traditional Mexican dishes.

However, they were also one of the products with the highest price volatility and seasonality. For example, tomatoes cost 40% more in August than in July, according to one commentator. Of course, if this kind of price volatility tends to skew the inflation numbers, then it has to be asked what the real impact would be? In August, consumer prices rose 0.55% above the expectations of 0.46%. Was that difference of 0.09% statistically significant?

Venezuela Attempts To Rein In Inflation Through A Cryptocurrency

Venezuela's president Nicolás Maduro announced in August 2018 a single exchange rate pegged to his socialist government's "Petro" cryptocurrency. In a country already impacted by dramatically rising prices, the move was destined, according to some commentators, to result in the effective devaluation of the Venezuelan Peso by over 90% and was a precursor to launch real hyperinflation. At one point, President Maduro said that he would introduce an increase in the minimum wage of over 3,000%. He said that he would also increase the corporate tax rate and raise the price of the highly subsidized gas prices. *"I want the country to recover and I have the formula. Trust me,"* he said. There were doubts that the country, which had already defaulted on its bonds, would succeed. One economist called these moves the worst of both worlds, with an aggressive devaluation and monetary expansions resulting in a much higher stage of hyperinflation. The International Monetary Fund predicted that inflation in Venezuela would hit one million percent. The opposition leader Henrique Capriles tweeted: *"No Venezuelan deserves to live this tragedy that these incapable people destroy our nation!"* Maduro said that he would be "Petrolizing" so that disparate exchange rates, salaries, pensions, and prices would be pegged to the Petro, the cryptocurrency. Cryptocurrency experts cast doubt on the Petro as a functional financial instrument, citing a lack of clear details on how it operated and US sanctions that made it off-limits. President Donald Trump had, in March, signed an executive order barring any US-based financial transactions involving the Petro, with officials warning that the

Venezuelan cryptocurrency was a scam. Venezuela's government didn't provide information regarding the names of the investors in the Petro and how much had been collected from sales of the cryptocurrency. Maduro said his plan would end the "tyranny" of the Dollar and lead to an economic rebirth in Venezuela, which was home to one of the world's largest crude oil reserves. Economists pointed to Venezuela's strict currency controls, botched nationalizations, and excessive money creation as the root causes of the country's economic crisis. Maduro said that one Petro would equal $60 and have the equivalent of 360 million Bolivars. That implied a new exchange rate of six million Bolivars per Dollar, close to the then black-market rate, which was about a 96% devaluation. He said *"They've dollarized our prices. I am petrolizing salaries and petrolizing prices. … We are going to convert the Petro into the reference that pegs the entire economy's movements."* Anyone following the Venezuelan economy after that will know that the outcome of these policies was not good.

Fed Up

In her book, *Fed Up,* Danielle DiMartino Booth made a number of incisive comments regarding the US Federal Reserve's use of inflation numbers, pointing out how very important decisions were being made based on those numbers and the selective use of certain categories of inflation like the "core" inflation index, which resulted in wrong decisions. In one chapter she mentioned how one of the Fed's Board members *"... had real problems with the Fed's designated measure of inflation,"* the "core" personal consumption expenditures (PCE) numbers, which ignored the prices of food and energy and thus did not reflect inflation's true level. *"But what prices do people remember most? What do they pay for gasoline at the pump and the price of a gallon of milk? Any elevation of those prices signaled to consumers that inflation was rising. By ignoring those trends, the Fed erodes its credibility."*

Inflation Numbers Knock-on Effect

Inflation numbers have a knock-on effect. For example, the US federal budget is greatly influenced by the Consumer Price Index (CPI). Just a small reduction in the annual CPI growth rate would reduce the government's deficit by tens of billions of dollars. In 1995, the US Federal Budget Office estimated that just a half percent reduction in the CPI annual growth rate starting in 1996 would reduce the Federal deficit in 2000 by $26 billion, simply because lower inflation expectations would enable the government to avoid raising the rate of interest in an effort to control inflation. I will discuss more on this in connection with the Boskin Commission.

Wage indexing

Over the years, politicians have advocated linking a legally mandated minimum wage to the consumer price index, thereby increasing wages automatically each year based on increases to the CPI. In the US in 1998, Washington State became the first state to approve linking the minimum wage to consumer prices. Later, other states like Oregon and Florida followed, as well as cities such as San Francisco and Santa Fe.

When Central Bank Actions Fail To Influence Inflation

Central banks pay close attention to the measured inflation rate on which they base critical decisions regarding money supply and interest rates. In the early 2000s, central banks of Japan, the US, and EU engaged in dramatically increased money printing, expanding their balance sheets to unprecedented levels by issuing cash to purchase bonds and other assets in order to induce inflation and inflation expectations based on the theory that this would create more economic activity and growth. However, the inflation index did not respond. They were not certain of the reason. Was it because the inflation index was not measuring the right things; or because people were not responding to what the central bank was doing?

The economic consensus was that inflation was necessary for a healthy economy since the labor market did not immediately adjust for the higher inflation, thus enabling businesses to benefit from a lower real cost of labor. Central banks thus have tried to influence inflation by manipulating interest rates, engaging in market operations by buying assets with newly issued currency, and adjusting the reserve requirements of banks down, since such a reduction would encourage banks to expand lending and thus increase the supply of credit into the economy. Of course, these actions have not always worked the way they were expected to work.

Investment Decisions and Inflation Numbers

Major investors who allocate large amounts of money watch the CPI and make snap decisions that can result in gains or losses of billions of dollars. The *Wall Street Journal* headline in early November 2016 read: "Inflation Fear Fuels Bond Rout." The article pointed to how rich country government bond prices were tumbling as a result of the high inflation statistics and the expectation that bond yields would rise in response. Previously, investors were worried about deflation, but now the worry was about inflation. As the bond prices tumbled, the yields on government bonds rose in line with the decline of their prices. Billions of dollars in losses and gains were involved based not on the information the investors researched themselves, but instead on statistics published by a government agency – which could have published inaccurate numbers. Bond buyers and sellers make those calculations and the result can be the gain or loss of billions of dollars for the bondholder.

Bank Decisions

Inflation numbers also have an impact on how interest rates are adjusted by banks. Calculations of the "real" interest rate (the interest rate minus the inflation rate) are important to lenders and borrowers. If the inflation numbers are rising, lenders want to raise their lending rates so they will not be disadvantaged with a loss in purchasing power of the interest they receive. If the lender – a bank or finance company – has entered into an adjustable rate loan where the interest rate is adjusted in line with inflation, then the CPI will determine the interest rate rise. If the loan is at a fixed rate, the lender will often include an "inflation risk premium" to the fixed interest rate loan based on the expectation of future inflation as measured by the CPI.

Summary

What these examples show is that no government is immune to inflation statistics. The "tyranny of inflation," as Aldrick aptly puts it, is a global phenomenon. Around the world politicians and central banks are basing important decisions on inflation numbers. And the measures taken as a result of this can have an enormous impact on peoples' lives. Therefore, it is absolutely crucial that the numbers we measure are correct.

3 What is Inflation?

Inflation is a phenomenon of currency, as I have pointed out, and is subject to extreme fluctuations as a result of changes, mostly increases, made by the issuing authorities. We measure inflation by how many units of a currency are necessary to purchase something – a product or service. If someone finds that it takes more units of currency to purchase the same product that he purchased yesterday at fewer units of the currency, then he would say that he is a victim of inflation.

Some people have described inflation as a balloon that expands as it is inflated, just as prices expand when inflation occurs. It can impact the price of one item or a whole set of items. Different economic theories have been formulated to explain inflation. Keynesian economists subscribe to the idea that when the total demand for goods and services exceeds supply, then there is inflation. Monetarists say that when there is an excess of money supply, the excess money causes inflation of assets, goods, and services. Another theory says that inflation is transmitted through international supply networks. Still, another theory says that when governments absorb all the resources with excess spending and borrowing, inflation follows.

What the Experts Say

Many famous economists, writers, politicians, and entertainers have made comments about inflation with dramatically different perspectives. Here's a summary of their ideas along with their words.

Inflation is Used by Government to Tax the People

*Milton Friedman, economist: *"Inflation is taxation without legislation."*[8]

*John Maynard Keynes, economist: *"By a continuing process of inflation, government can confiscate, secretly and unobserved, an important part of the wealth of their citizens."*[9]

*Thomas Sowell, senior fellow at the Hoover Institution, Stanford University: *"It is a way to take people's wealth from them without having to openly raise taxes. Inflation is the most universal tax of all."*[10]

*Friedrich August von Hayek, economist: *"I do not think it is an exaggeration to say history is largely a history of inflation, usually inflations engineered by governments for the gain of governments."*[2]

*Ayn Rand, developer of the philosophical system Objectivism: *"Inflation is not caused by the actions of private citizens, but by the government: by an artificial expansion of the money supply required to support deficit spending. No private embezzlers or bank robbers in history have ever plundered people's savings on a scale comparable to the plunder perpetrated by the fiscal policies of statist governments."*[11]

Inflation is Used by Governments to Solve Budget Deficits and Pay Their Debts

Ernest Hemingway, novelist and journalist: *"The first panacea for a mismanaged nation is inflation of the currency; the second is war. Both bring a temporary prosperity; both bring a permanent ruin. But both are the refuge of political and economic opportunists."*[12]

Herbert Hoover, 31st president of the United States: *"There are only three ways to meet the unpaid bills of a nation. The first is taxation. The second is repudiation. The third is inflation."*[3]

*Sri Mulyani Indrawati, minister of finance of Indonesia: *"Many emerging countries are facing the same issue of overheating and inflation because they have been vigorously expanding fiscal and monetary policy to counter the 2008 shock."*[14]

*James Callaghan, former UK prime minister *"We used to think that you could spend your way out of a recession and increase employment by cutting taxes and boosting government spending. I tell you in all candor that the option no longer exists, and in so far as it ever did exist, it only worked on each occasion since the war by injecting a bigger dose of inflation into the economy, followed by a higher level of unemployment as the next step."*[15]

Companies Maintain Profits By Increasing Prices

*W. Edwards Deming, developer of the sampling techniques used by the US Department of the Census and the Bureau of Labor Statistics: *"Declining productivity and quality means your unit production costs stay high, but you don't have as much as to sell. Your workers don't want to be paid less, so to maintain profits, you increase your prices. That's inflation."*[16]

Governments Can Control Inflation

*Janet Yellen, former chair of the US Federal Reserve: *"Efforts to promote financial stability through* *adjustments in interest rates would increase the volatility of inflation and employment. As a result, I believe a macroprudential approach to supervision and regulation needs to play the primary role."*[17]

Increased Production Can Solve Inflation

Chester Bowles, former US ambassador to India: "Production is the only answer to inflation."[18]

Growth Can Be Achieved by Lower Inflation

*Raghuram Rajan, former governor of the Reserve Bank of India: *"I have said repeatedly that the way to sustainable growth is to bring down inflation to much more reasonable levels."*[19]

Inflation is Bad

*Milton Friedman, economist: *"Inflation is a disease, a dangerous and sometimes fatal disease, a disease that if not checked in time can destroy a society."*[20]

*Ludwig von Mises, Austrian School economist: *"Inflation is essentially antidemocratic."*[21] *"Continued inflation inevitably leads to catastrophe."*[22]

*Toba Beta, author: *"Inflation creates bubble and burst. That develops world economy and will destroy it too."*[23]

*Henry Hazlitt, business and economics journalist: *"Like every other tax, inflation acts to determine the individual and business policies we are all forced to follow. It discourages all prudence and thrift. It encourages squandering, gambling, reckless waste of all kind. It often makes it more profitable to speculate than to produce. It tears apart the whole fabric of stable economic relationships. Its inexcusable injustices drive men toward desperate remedies. It plants the seeds of fascism and communism. It leads men to demand totalitarian controls. It ends invariably in bitter disillusion and collapse."*[24]

*Kevin Brady, US congressman and chairman of the House Ways and Means Committee: *"Inflation destroys savings, impedes planning, and discourages investment. That means less productivity and a lower standard of living."*[25]

*Azim Premji, chairman of Wipro Limited: *"Inflation is taking up the poverty line, and poverty is not just economic but defined by way of health and education."*[26]

Inflation Must Be Defeated

*Paul Samuelson, father of modern economics: *"Avoiding inflation is not an absolute imperative, but rather is one of a number of conflicting goals that we* *must pursue and that we may often have to compromise.*"[27]

*Martin Feldstein, president emeritus of the National Bureau of Economic Research: *"Thirty years ago, many economists argued that inflation was a kind of minor inconvenience and that the cost of reducing inflation was too high a price to pay. No one would make those arguments today."*[28]

People Spend in Order to Defeat Inflation

*Robert Kiyosaki, founder of Rich Dad Company: *"People concerned about inflation today tend to buy big houses and nice cars."*[29]

Inflation Destroys Your Savings

*Robert Orben, former head speechwriter to former Vice President Gerald R. Ford: *"Inflation is the crabgrass in your savings."*[30]

Inflation is Good

*Ha-Joon Chang, South Korean institutional economist: *"Low inflation and government prudence may be harmful for economic development." "There is a big logical jump between acknowledging the destructive nature of hyperinflation and arguing that the lower the rate of inflation, the better."*[31]

*Jerome Powell, chairman of the US Federal Reserve: *"Below-target inflation increases the real value of debts owed by households and businesses and reduces the ability of central banks to respond to downturns."*[32]

*Janet Yellen, former chair of the US Federal Reserve: *"To me, a wise and humane policy is occasionally to let inflation rise even when inflation is running above target."*[33]

*Ben Bernanke, former chairman of the US Federal Reserve: *"Low and stable inflation in many counties is an important accomplishment that will continue to bring significant benefits."*[34] *"The US government has a technology, called the printing press (or, today, the electronic equivalent) that allows it to produce as many US dollars as it wishes at essentially no cost. ... We conclude that under a paper money system, a determined government can always generate higher spending and hence positive inflation ... through its ability to print money the government can create inflation and that's a good thing."*[35]

*Milton Friedman, economist: *"Inflation is always and everywhere a monetary phenomenon in the sense that it is and can be produced only by a more rapid increase in the quantity of money than in output. A steady rate of monetary growth at a moderate level can provide a framework under which a country can have little inflation and much growth. It will not produce *perfect stability; it will not produce heaven on earth; but it can make an important contribution to a stable economic society."*

Inflation is Caused by Too Much Money

*Robert Kiyosaki, founder of Rich Dad Company: *"In the simplest terms, inflation occurs when there's too much money in the system."*[36]

*Henry Hazlitt, business and economics journalist: *"Mere inflation – that is, the mere issuance of more money, with the consequence of higher wages and prices – may look like the creation of more demand. But in terms of the actual production and exchange of real things it is not."*[37]

Central Bankers Must Control Inflation

*James Surowiecki, former staff writer at *The New Yorker: "Of course, looking tough on inflation is part of any central banker's job description: if investors believe that inflation is going to get out of control, you end up with higher interest rates and capital flight, and a vicious circle quickly ensues."*[38]

Central Banks Cause Inflation

*Jim Powell, senior fellow at the Cato Institute: *"The great majority of central banks were established after*

1900 to help governments spend money they didn't have. They became engines of inflation. The largest number of runaway inflations and the worst runaway inflations have occurred since 1900."[39]

Businesses Raise Prices in Anticipation of Inflation

*James Surowiecki, former staff writer at *The New Yorker*: "Businesses that have gone through an episode of hyperinflation become understandably alert to the threat of it: at the first hint of inflation, they're likely to increase prices, since they've learned that if they don't, and inflation hits, their businesses will be wrecked.*"[40]

Higher Inflation and Higher Interest Rates are a Vicious Cycle

*Arundhati Bhattacharya, former chairman of the State Bank of India: *"The higher interest and higher inflation is a vicious cycle.*"[41]

Inflation is Related to a High Government Debt and Low Growth

*Bill Gross, fixed income investment manager: *"Slow growth and inflation have a tendency to accompany large deficits and increasing debt as a percentage of GDP.*"[42]

Budget Deficits Do Not Cause Inflation

*William Vickrey, professor of economics and Nobel Laureate: *"Deficits do not in themselves produce inflation, nor does a balanced budget assure a stable price level."*[43]

Inflation is Caused by Higher Labor Costs

*Douglas R. Oberhelman, former CEO and executive chairman of Caterpillar Inc.: *"Inflation was driven by higher labor costs, not higher goods costs. Frankly, I'd love to see a little bit of that. Because I'd love to pay people more. I'd love to see rising wages for everybody."*[44]

Rising Prices Do Not Cause Inflation but Only Report It

*Walter Bigelow Wriston, former president and chairman of Citibank: *"Rising prices do not cause inflation; they only report it. They represent an essential form of economic speech, since money is just another form of information."*[45]

Inflation is Not the Increase in the Quantity of Money

*Ludwig von Mises, Austrian School economist: *"What people today call inflation is not inflation, i.e., the increase in the quantity of money and money substitutes, but the general rise in commodity prices and wage rates which is the inevitable consequence of inflation."*[46]

Defining Inflation

As can be seen by those quotes, views on inflation are highly varied and often conflicting. However, there is a basic consensus that inflation is a measurement based on recording the change in prices of a wide variety of goods and services. In order to simplify the process, an index is constructed to reflect the overall change in value. This then is considered representative of the general state of prices. A number of different price indices have been created, but the Consumer Price Index (CPI) has been the premier index to measure annual price changes since it is supposed to be a reflection of the impact of changing prices on the entire population. Of course, such a measure is an enormous simplification.

When defining inflation, we must reflect on the various theories surrounding the concept. The "Quantity Theory of Inflation" suggests that inflation is caused by an increase in the supply of money or "monetary inflation," but it has become clear that a rise in the supply of money may or may not result in higher prices. So, the search by economists to track the causes of inflation continues. One theory called the "Quality Theory" is based on a seller's expectation that he will be able to use a given amount of currency to purchase the same goods or services in the future. If a seller thinks more money will be required to purchase that same product in the future, then he will inflate his selling price.

Another explanation is called "Demand-Pull" inflation, where an increase in demand as a result of a rise in private and government spending leads to inflation. This kind of inflation is seen as beneficial to economic growth since the excess demand combined with favorable market conditions leads to more investment and expansion.

Inflation following a fall in the supply of goods and services resulting in higher raw materials prices is called "Cost-Push" inflation. Sometimes, if there is a natural disaster that restricts supplies, the more dramatic name "Supply Shock Inflation" is used. Then there is "Built-In Inflation" when higher prices are the result of, for example, suppliers raising prices when the inflation-linked contracts that they have with their workers force them to raise wages. In these instances, it is called the "Price/ Wage Spiral." Finally, there is "Asset Price Inflation" – a rise in the prices of financial assets.

Inflation as a Worldwide Disaster

In 1973, Irving Friedman, an economist and university professor, wrote a book called *Inflation: A Worldwide Disaster*. In it, he said that during the preceding 30 years, country after country had tried to cope with the problem of continuously rising prices and wages. Although there were temporary successes, the general record was one of repeated failures. Governments had proved incapable of providing solutions that were politically and socially acceptable. Instead they pursued policies that strengthened inflationary trends that led to a nearly universal conviction that inflation was inevitable and that governments could not or should not bring rising price trends to an end.

In the book, Friedman did an historical analysis of inflation and how in the sixteenth-century European society it was impacted by large increases in gold and silver imports from the New World to Spain that found their way to other countries in Europe, leading to higher prices and higher interest rates. That resulted in the Catholic Church raising a voice about usurious interest rates and what was a "just" or fair price.

He said that the problem is societal and therefore solutions have to deal with social causes and cannot be left only to the economists. Like other observers of so-called inflation, he stated that inflation fell most heavily on the poorest. This, of course, led to a logical conclusion that the government must step in and take action.

Price behavior in the 1960s showed that the average price increase for a sample of 37 developing countries was about 3.5% per year, or a doubling in prices every 20 years. The countries Friedman was talking about included Mexico, Guatemala, Costa Rica, Pakistan, Thailand, Korea, Indonesia, Brazil, Chile, and Argentina;

currency printing in some of these countries was rife and of course led to prices becoming somewhat meaningless. Friedman repeated the oft-mentioned theory that when more money chased fewer goods, the purchasing power of money falls so that market forces drive prices up. In his book, he said that he believed that the world was entering a period in which the pace of the persistent inflation would become so disruptive as to force its recognition and solution. He said that persistent inflation could not be expected to be self-correcting.

In describing how consumer prices were measured, Irving Friedman identified the failure of such statistics since they were a simplification of the average prices paid by consumers for all goods and services. The weights given to the relative importance of different goods and services differed among consumers. The "average" did not reflect what most people experienced and there were substantial differences for various parts of the country.

Summary

The fact that there are so many differing and even contrary theories on inflation from eminent economists, in my opinion, reflects our general ignorance of what inflation is and what effect it is actually having on our economies. Therefore, it should not come as a surprise that governments and policymakers time and again struggle when dealing with this phenomenon. Definitions are vague and so is our approach to measurement, as we will see in the following chapters. The problem is, when it comes to inflation we cannot just rely on the largest common denominator, we have to be as concise and accurate as possible. The implications of political decisions based on inflation numbers are too far-reaching.

4 What is Hyperinflation?

There is no precise definition of hyperinflation simply because, when it occurs, all measurement can be thrown out of the window – even though people will still try to measure it. It can be best described as out-of-control inflation where price increases are so wild, they defy imagination. In the twentieth century, It is estimated that hyperinflation occurred over 50 times during the twentieth century, for example in China, Germany, Russia, Brazil, Hungary, Argentina, Venezuela, and other countries. Monetarists would say that it happens when a big increase in money supply is not matched by the gross national product growth. But perhaps a better description would be when people lose all faith in a currency and try to get rid of it as fast as possible by converting it into real goods. Then, hoarding begins to take place as people see goods as a store of value rather than money as a store of value. Panic sets in and excessive demand pushes prices up dramatically. Goods leave the shops so quickly that the shelves are empty. In real terms, tax revenues decline, and then the reaction of the government is often to simply print more currency to meet government expenditures.

What the Experts Say

A number of writers and economists have talked about hyperinflation. This is what they have to say:

*Chuck Grassley, US senator: *"The Fed has the ability to put money out, it's got the ability to take money back in, and if they don't do that, we will have hyperinflation worse than we had in 1980 and 1981."*[47]

*Thomas Sowell, economist: *"Hyperinflation can take virtually your entire life's savings, without the government having to bother raising the official tax rate at all."*[48]

*Timothy Geithner, former US treasury secretary: *"Hyperinflation is not going to happen in this country, will never happen. . . The Fed putting so much money into the system is not going to create the risk of hyperinflation in the future. We have a strong independent Federal Reserve with a very strong mandate from the*

Congress, and they will do what's necessary to keep inflation low and stable over time."[49]

*Laurence Kotlikoff, economics professor at Boston University: *"The United States has experienced high rates of inflation in the past and appears to be running the same type of fiscal policies that engendered hyperinflations in 20 countries over the past century."*[50]

*Henry Hazlitt, business and economics journalist: *"The monetary managers are fond of telling us that they have substituted 'responsible money management' for the gold standard. But there is no historic record of responsible paper money management . . . The record taken, as a whole is one of hyperinflation, devaluation and monetary chaos."*[51]

*Llewellyn Rockwell, author: *"The Fed is pushing a variety of workarounds that would inject trillions in new money into the economy while bypassing the banking system altogether. Time will tell whether or not this will succeed. Meanwhile, a serious danger lurks around the corner. Once the recession is over, the lending will start again. With fractional-reserve banking and limitless supplies of cash on hand, we will likely see the overall price trends reversed, from deflation to inflation to possible hyperinflation."*[52]

*James Surowiecki, journalist: *"Businesses that have gone through an episode of hyperinflation become understandably alert to the threat of it: at the first hint of inflation, they're likely to increase prices, since they've learned that if they don't, and inflation hits, their businesses will be wrecked."*[40]

Hyperinflations around the World

Hyperinflations have been studied extensively by Steve Hanke and Nicholas Krus of Johns Hopkins University. As of December 2016, they identified 17 hyperinflationary periods in 16 countries in the period from 1922 to 2007, including Hungary, Zimbabwe, France, Ukraine, Germany, Greece, China, Armenia, and others. Daily inflation rates in these cases ranged from a low of 5% to a high of 98%. The time it took for prices to double ranged from 15 hours in the case of Hungary in 1945 to 16 days in Poland in 1923. Of course, key to this kind of inflation were the currencies that lost all credibility, such as the Hungarian Pengo, German Papiermark, Taiwan Yen, and Poland Marka, which disappeared off the pages of history.

The German Hyperinflation Experience

In his excellent 1975 book *When Money Dies,* Adam Fergusson wrote about the nightmare of deficit spending, devaluation, and hyperinflation in Weimar Germany.

In the preface of the book, he said that comparisons of contemporary prices and values with those a half-century earlier was of a limited advantage, since after 35 years, currencies have continually merged, diverged, depreciated, or even disappeared. Costs and wages have risen and fallen with so little uniformity that the exercise sheds no light. He said that although money may not any longer be physically printed and distributed in the incredible quantities of 1923 Germany, "quantitative easing" – a modern euphemism for surreptitious deficit spending in the electronic era – is also an assault on monetary discipline. Whatever the cause of the country's deficit, respected leaders still believe that the printing press is the best last resort to balance a government budget despite the impact it has on people's savings and pensions – as well as their confidence and trust. One of the best lessons was Germany after the First World War. It demonstrated that as people's trust in their currency declines, they spend faster, the velocity of circulation increases, prices take off, and more money is needed. In Germany, the disaster could best be illustrated by the fact that in 1923, one British Shilling could be exchanged for one billion German Marks.

For the Germans, perhaps their biggest mistake was their belief in the German Mark. Most of them kept on believing in the Mark even after they saw its value crashing. So when prices went up, people did not demand a stable purchasing power for their Marks, instead demanding more Marks to buy what they needed. Therefore, more Marks were printed without constraint, resulting in the complete destruction of the currency and people's confidence in it. At any time that kind of trust can decline and people's trust in currencies wane as news about foreign-exchange fluctuations and global travel, as well as global instant news, bring the reality of a weak currency quickly to the fore.

In post-First World War Germany, the decision by the government to pay for the crushing war reparations by printing money was the key error leading to hyperinflation. But unlike the present day and age, Germans, with the exception of the very few who were knowledgeable, were sheltered from the information pointing to their beloved Mark's depreciation. During the war, the German stock exchange was closed, so the effect of the Reichsbank policies on bonds and shares was unknown. Also, foreign exchange rates were not published, so unless you were in contact with outside neutral markets – such as Amsterdam or Zurich – you couldn't know what was going on. It may be said that the prelude to the post-war hyperinflation came during the war when consumer goods were in short supply and black market prices were skyrocketing. Then the Versailles peace terms imposed a huge debt burden on Germany and set the next stage for a currency catastrophe when the German government decided to print more currency to pay its debts.

It's important to note that even in these disastrous inflationary conditions – that left many destitute as their earnings and savings evaporated – in terms of purchasing power, there were some winners. Black market operators, smugglers, and other speculators were having a field day, as portrayed in the Greta Garbo film *The Joyless Streets* which portrayed the misery as well as the cafes full of merrymakers. When, after the war, stock exchanges opened up, there were opportunities to keep pace with inflation by converting the depreciating currency into shares of companies whose prices were shooting up. Those who were willing to break the law and convert their Marks into Swiss Francs also were able to preserve their wealth. Businesses created balances abroad in foreign currencies by under-invoicing their exports and asking their customers abroad to deposit the difference in banks overseas.

US Dollars, Swiss Francs, and Dutch Guilders were the most favored foreign currencies, but Czech Crowns were also popular. Credits in Swiss banks in Dutch names were out of proportion to the trade between the Netherlands and Switzerland, suggesting surreptitious operations to evade government controls. The assumption was that the Germans were hiding behind Dutch names. Also benefiting were those foreigners buying up real property and shares of factories with foreign currency.

Hugo Stinnes, considered the richest and most powerful industrialist in Germany, had a business empire estimated to have included over one-sixth of the country's industry, which was to a great extent built on the foundation of the inflationary situation. He said that inflation was something desirable and was the only means of guaranteeing employment for the people.

German countryside landowners and farmers were less affected since they were producing most of their own essentials and raising market prices as much as the shopkeepers. Those with mortgages to pay were enormously benefited, since they could pay in the continually devaluing currency. In one case, in June of 1922, a speculator purchased 100 tons of maize from a dealer for eight million marks and a week later, before it was even delivered, he sold the whole load back to the same dealer for double the amount, making a huge profit. He used the money to furnish the mansion of his new estate with antique furniture. If this wasn't enough, he then bought three guns, six suits and three of the most expensive pairs of shoes in Berlin, all before spending eight days enjoying himself in the city. Many were safeguarding themselves against losses in paper currency by buying assets which could retain their value, such as houses, equipment, raw materials, etc. But those on fixed salaries or those who were not savvy enough to move to hard assets suffered greatly.

After the end of the Second World War in 1945, the command economy continued under the occupation forces as the ravages of war were gradually forgotten and stability returned. Within ten years, inflation had come down to a single-digit level. After 1957, inflation in Germany did not exceed 8% and for most years following this it was at single-digit levels. In the 30-year period from 1957 to 1987, the German consumer price index ranged between a high of 8% to deflation of less than zero. In the next 30-year cycle from 1987 to 2017, inflation ranged up to a high of a little more than 6% and in a number of cases was less than zero. The most important development regarding inflation in Germany came when the Euro was introduced at the beginning of 1999. Actual euro notes and coins began to circulate in 2002 and Germany replaced the Mark with the euro. Initially, when the introduction of a common European currency was being negotiated in the early 1990s, Germany was cautious about approving it since the Mark had proven to be so stable and there were still memories of the hyperinflation that the country had experienced. One hurdle was the requirement that any state joining the new currency union had to have a budget deficit of less than 3% of their GDP, a debt ratio of less than 60% of GDP, a low inflation rate, and an interest rate near the EU average. This set the stage for further discipline on government spending for all the nations who wanted to adopt the new currency. Germany was one of the first nations to embrace the new currency and the Mark officially was no longer legal tender on 31 December 2001. So, in 2018, anyone less than 60 years of age had lived through a period of relatively stable prices, even though they may have heard from their parents about the terrible inflation in the past. And in 2018, inflation was running at an average of less than 2%.

Yugoslavia: Printing Money To Pay Government Debt

In August of 1989, it was reported that Yugoslavia was planning to introduce a new currency in order to fight inflation, which had reached almost 800%. The previous re-denomination of the currency in 1965 replaced 100 Old Dinars for 1 New Dinar. The exchange rate against the US Dollar had collapsed from 3,000 a year previously to 28,900. The national bank had printed a new 500,000-Dinar bill but it was already worth less than 17 US Dollars. The bank was then preparing a 1-million-Dinar note.

Since the country was nearing a complete breakup into opposing states, it had already been experiencing inflation at rates that exceeded 75% annually. Then it was found that the Serbian province leader had robbed the national treasury by issuing $1.5 billion of loans to his friends and associates. The result was that the government, in an effort to meet debt obligations, started printing excessive amounts of cash.

Hyperinflation quickly developed, such that the rate of price increases practically doubled each day. At one point, it reached the rate of 300 million percent a month. The result was chaos with people abandoning the currency and bartering for goods. The government then finally replaced the currency with the German Mark so that the situation could be stabilized.

It was a nightmare for shoppers who had to struggle with the daily devaluation of their banknotes and accountants who were dealing with figures too big for their pocket calculators.

Legalized Looting In Zimbabwe

In November 2007, it was reported that Zimbabwe could no longer calculate the rate of inflation because, as a result of hoarding and people's efforts to get rid of the devaluing currency as fast as possible, there were not enough goods left in the shops to allow price comparisons. The director of the Central Statistical Office (CSO), Moffat Nyoni, said that it had been impossible to compile reliable data for the previous month because of the unavailability of required information, such as prices of goods, due to their shortage on the formal market. In November, leaks from the CSO indicated that inflation in October had reached 14,840% – almost double the 8,000% of September.

Because the government of Robert Mugabe had forced businesses to slash prices to below what it cost to buy or produce goods, store shelves were quickly being emptied. In addition, business people were being arrested for "overcharging" and were being raided by soldiers, police, and state secret agents in an orgy of legalized looting.

By February of 2008, the governor of the Reserve Bank of Zimbabwe announced that the official inflation number for November 2007 had reached 26,470%. He also announced a 2007 shrinkage in the economy by 6%. He criticized the government for not releasing inflation statistics in a timely manner to preserve credibility and enable proper business planning. Because of the difficulties of measuring the value of Zimbabwe's currency due to ongoing hyperinflation, people reverted to the Old Mutual Implied Rate (OMIR). Old Mutual is a South African insurance company that trades at the Harare, London and Johannesburg stock exchanges. Inflation numbers and exchange rate changes are estimated based on a comparison of the stock prices of OMIR in London and Harare. It was not a good sign, therefore, that the Zimbabwean government was considering measures to eliminate the OMIR and suspend trading of Old Mutual shares in Harare in June 2020. At that point, inflation numbers in Zimbabwe showed an annual rate of almost 800%.

Printing 30 Tons of Zairean Banknotes

In 1995, Zaire's inflation was running at a yearly rate of 9,000%, which was some improvement on the previous year as a result of the government restricting the supply of money. But there were problems in implementing the restrictions on cash, since at Kinshasa's airport a plane was discovered carrying 30 tons of Zairean banknotes ordered by corrupt government officials and bankers. Each series of the banknotes had been reprinted at least five times. Their plan was to channel the notes into black-markets. Arrests were made, but then a sudden restriction of issuing cash into the economy meant that banks were starved of liquidity and unable to function, so civil servants and army staff were not getting paid.

Summary

Responsible government policy is essential when it comes to monetary measures. People need to be able to trust their governments to make the right decisions. Reckless measures can have disastrous consequences for businesses and individuals and, in the worst case scenario, lead to hyperinflation. This phenomenon, as we have seen, can wipe out lifetime savings within a few days and lead to political instability. The next chapter will demonstrate that, while money printing might be costless for central banks, it can come at a high price for society. However, responsible monetary policies presuppose that politicians have the information they need to make the right decisions. But, of course, we know that they don't.

5 Money Supply and Inflation

Inflation as a Monetary Phenomenon

The monetarist Milton Friedman argued that *"inflation is always and everywhere a monetary phenomenon"*[28] and that inflation can and should be managed through central bank control of the amount of money in circulation. He said that inflation could be controlled by the central bank adopting a constant money growth rule; so, the higher the central bank wanted inflation, the higher the money growth rate should be

In the early 1980s, it was assumed that Paul Volcker, chairman of the Fed's Federal Open Market Committee, had reduced the inflation rate from about 10% to 3.5% through a reduction in the rate of money supply growth. But it was later found that the theory did not consistently work, and money growth targets were abandoned.

So, Friedman's theory, although widely popularized in his lifetime, was shown to be invalid. I remember hearing him talk to a packed audience in Hong Kong, where he expounded on his theories not only about money supply but free markets. At that time, he said that he considered Hong Kong to be one of the world's freest economies and pointed to it as an example for other countries to follow. Interestingly and significantly, the Hong Kong Dollar was pegged to the US Dollar – so Hong Kong was forced to be disciplined in their money supply policies.

What Is The Money Supply?

No one really knows what the world's supply of money is. The rise of cryptocurrencies is making the problem even more acute. Money supply data are recorded and published by governments, usually by the country's central bank. But they are at a loss to accurately measure other forms of currency used, such as cryptocurrencies and forms of digital exchange. The numbers issued by the central banks are carefully studied by many economists, but some have questioned the importance of money supply data to predict inflation. Instead, they say that inflation is found in the distribution structure of the economy. They also question measures taken regarding the money supply that may be the opposite of what is intended. They say that after a recession, when resources are underutilized, an increase in the money supply can cause a real increase in production but no inflation. Also, if the velocity of money, or the rate at which money is exchanged in an economy, undergoes a shift, any increase in the money supply may have no effect at all.

Measuring Money Supply

The difficulty in measuring money supply stems from its different functions. Money can be used in three ways: as a medium of exchange; as a unit of account; or as a store of value. Hence, money supply has been measured in different ways on a spectrum from "narrow" to "broad". In the past, the amount of paper or coin currency in circulation was relatively easy to measure. But with the development of a sophisticated banking system, demand deposits in banks and other financial institutions had to be considered. Its measurement became more important as "quantity theory of money" proponents found evidence of a direct relationship between growth of the money supply and prices in the economy. Thus the search for a comprehensive accounting method had to consider further elements: central bank money, which included currency and central bank deposit accounts; commercial bank money, which included obligations of commercial banks such as checking and savings accounts; and more.

There are several approaches to measuring the money supply, from "narrow" to "broad." The narrow approach focuses only on the most liquid assets or the ones most easily used for spending. These would include actual currency and checking deposits. The broader measures would include all kinds of assets, such as certificates of deposit, in addition to the narrow money supply items. Economists debate what definition of money is most useful for policy actions and which have the most important effect.

The different types of money are typically classified as "M"s. The "M"s usually range from M0 (narrowest) to M3 (broadest).

Money Creation through Fractional-Reserve Banking

The difficulty of assessing exactly how much money is in the system is exacerbated by the fractional-reserve banking system where banks have in their vaults only a fraction of what they are lending. The degree to which banks are aggressive in lending determines how much money is being used in the system. In a fractional-reserve banking system, where only a fraction of bank deposits are backed by actual cash on hand and available for withdrawal with a multiple of deposits lent to customers, central bank decisions on what multiple of deposits can be lent out will determine the amount of money in circulation to some extent; but the individual banks' decisions regarding how aggressively they would like to create loans will also be a key determinant of how much money is circulating in the economy. This process is impossible to measure precisely and in a timely manner.

Central banks try to regulate money supply by implementing policies of "easy money," or "tightening." In the "easy money" scenario, central banks create new bank reserves allowing the banks to lend more. As these loans get spent, they are deposited in other banks and whatever is not required to be held as reserves is then lent out again. There is thus a multiplying effect, so that the loans and bank deposits go up by many times as the initial injection of reserves. But when the central bank is tightening, it sells securities such as government bonds thus extracting cash from the system. In order to loosen, it reverses the process and buys back the bonds and other securities, thus enabling them to pour cash back into the system. As you can imagine, the process is quite imprecise and its impact difficult – if not impossible – to measure.

In the late 1900s, a popular debate among economists was about central banks' ability to predict the amount of money that should be put into circulation to create specific employment and inflation rate levels. Despite their faith in money supply regulation, economists such as Milton Friedman believed that the central bank would always get it wrong and it would be better to not try to regulate the money supply based on changing economic statistics such as the inflation rate. He and others advocated a non-interventionist approach where a pre-specified money supply path, independent of the prevailing economic conditions, would be best.

The Money Illusion

In his book *The Money Illusion* published in 1928, Irving Fisher tried to show how unstable in buying power all kinds of money were, including the US dollar. Even at a time when the dollar was fixed in terms of gold and redeemable in a fixed number of grains of gold, he pointed out that it was not fixed in the number of goods and benefits it could command. Therefore, there was a "safe money illusion." In the book, he stated the basic premise as follows: if the circulation of money increases relative to the circulation of goods, price levels rise. If, on the contrary, money supply decreases, price levels fall. In the first case, there is inflation; in the second, deflation; and the index of price reveals from time to time which of the two is going on, he said.

In the book, he made the case that *while "... the money stream is found to vary greatly, the goods stream varies comparatively little, especially per capita, that is, in relation to population."* Fisher did not deal with the fact that the "goods stream" is constantly changing, not only because of new products but also because of the change in quality and functionality of goods. Fisher did point out that if a man who previously received $2,000 a year now got $4,000 while the prices of all things he had to buy had doubled, he was no worse off and no better off than before. His present-day Dollar bought only half of what his former Dollar bought, but he now had $2 for every $1 before, so his real condition had not changed. This, of course, assumed that the quality and variety of the goods he was now buying was the same as before, which we all know is not the case.

Fisher talked about the impact of a weakening Dollar and a stronger Dollar. The Dollar that was being depreciated bought less than it had done 10 years previously, and it penalized bondholders because the value of the bond depreciated as a result of its declining value in terms of purchasing power. On the other side, however, the borrowers who had issued bonds and had to pay the interest on them were benefiting because the purchasing power of the interest payments was less. The conclusion then was that rising price levels as a result of monetary depreciation stimulated the economy, while monetary appreciation and falling price levels depressed business. The theory is that when producers get higher prices, they don't have to pay correspondingly higher costs since wages and salaries do not rise so fast being fixed by contract in advance. The same goes for rent and interest payments.

Credit Is Money

In his 1985 book, *Funny Money*, Mark Singer wrote
about the 1982 collapse of Penn Square Bank in
Oklahoma City. It shocked America's banking industry
and led eventually to the failure of one of America's
largest banks, Continental Illinois Bank. It was a time,
by the end of 1982, when US banks had too many
deposits and were lending billions of Dollars to countries which at the time were considered risky, such as
Mexico, Brazil, Venezuela, Argentina, and others. At one
point, the ten largest banks in the United States had
more than one and a half times their equity value in
loans to less-developed countries. It was also a time
when banks were lending aggressively to the oil and gas
industry with oil prices high and rising. But this led to
reckless lending and smaller banks like Penn Square
selling participation in their loans to larger banks like
Continental Illinois. Soon, undocumented collateral and
sloppy paperwork loans were made simply on the signa-
ture of someone the banker knew in his bank's head-
quarters in Oklahoma City. The demise of one bank in
1984 resulted in upstream banks charging off more than
half of their loans worth more than $1 billion. This was
basically money that had been created by the banks and
now was gone. In the case of Continental Illinois in
1984, the bank's books showed that the bank had lost
$1.2 billion. This story and the story of many other

bank failures is a testament to the fact that money can be created out of thin air and it's impossible to predict or ascertain from one day to the next what the real money supply is.

The Collapse of Paper Money

In his 2011 book *Paper Money Collapse: The Folly of Elastic Money and the Coming Monetary Breakdown,* Detlev S. Schlichter, an Austrian School economist and international financial investor, said that the root cause of instability in the financial system was caused by limitless paper money as opposed to commodity money like gold. He pointed out that throughout human history, paper money systems have either collapsed in chaos or society has returned to commodity money – usually based on gold – before a total currency disaster occurred. He said that paper money systems based on an elastic and constantly expanding supply of money (as opposed to a system of commodity money of essentially fixed supply) were inherently unstable and would lead to economic disorder. Advocates of paper money around the world, he said, were misguided, and particularly the policy of accelerated paper money production to stimulate the economy would lead to catastrophe. There was a historical fact that commodity money always provided a reasonably stable medium of exchange, while the entire history of state paper money

had been an unmitigated disaster when judged on the
basis of price level stability. He went on to say that
replacing inelastic commodity money with state-issued
paper money had for some time always resulted in rising
inflation.

Pointing to the financial crisis in 2008 and the
collapse of the investment bank Lehman Brothers, he
showed how the Federal Reserve had expanded the
money supply resulting in creating almost twice the
amount of money that the Fed had created since its
inception in 1913. The Fed, he wrote, had used
$1 trillion of new money to take on to its own balance
sheet chunks of toxic assets that were on bank balance
sheets as a result of bad lending decisions during the
preceding boom. He concluded that although money
printing might be costless to the Fed, it was not costless
to society. The most visible effect of elastic money was
ongoing inflation and the deterioration of the purchasing power of the monetary unit. Over the 50 years up
to the onset of the 2008 financial crisis, industrial
production in the United States had increased by a
factor of about 5, but over the same time period, the
amount of Dollar notes and coins in circulation
increased by a factor of 26 so that every Dollar lost
about 86% of its purchasing power. He explained that
most money was not only produced by the Federal
Reserve but by banks. The central bank extended a
license to banks to create specific forms of money, since

the money supply included currency in circulation, demand deposits at banks, various time deposits, money market funds, and other items. About 80% of that money was a balance sheet item at a bank. Those balance sheet positions were regarded as a form of money because the banks promised their customers to convert them upon demand into money proper. This fractional-reserve banking was a Ponzi scheme, he said. The depositors put their money holdings in the bank and got paper receipts in return. They knew the banker would issue more receipts as part of his lending business so that, ultimately, considerably more paper tickets circulated than there was money in the bank to pay out every holder of the paper ticket. However, the banker shared some of his profit from this process of money creation with his depositors, which was their incentive to participate in this game.

Demise of the Dollar

In the book *The Demise of the Dollar* and his paper *Short Unhappy Episodes in Monetary History,* Addison Wiggin pointed to the ninth-century China "flying money" (mentioned previously), which the Chinese gave up after several hundred years because it proved to be subject to political whims and gave rise to disastrous consumer price inflation. He wrote that the same theme of "elastic money," where there is an ever-increasing supply of

money, would lead to inflation in modern times. Other
examples cited were France in 1717–29 under John Law's
scheme where paper money lost 90% of its value; Abe
Lincoln's financing of the Civil War which sparked
inflation that resulted in Americans rejecting paper
money until 1913; Peron's Argentinian coup in 1943
which introduced more paper money than the country's
gold reserve. Then there was the Weimar-era hyperinflation we have discussed.

The Gold Standard

In 1821, countries began a systematic program to value
their currencies in gold. The British Pound Sterling's
value was set at a quarter of an ounce of gold and 1 US
Dollar was set at 1/20th of an ounce. In Japan, the Meiji
government set 1-Yen worth at about 1.5 grams of pure
gold. This set system of valuation enabled exchange rates
to be fixed in gold value. But the problem came when
the government was not able to support all the money
they printed with gold reserves. Soon, gold mining
production could not keep up with the printing of
money required for the First World War arms race. With
the US Dollar tied to gold reserves, the British Pound
was then tied to gold and Dollars, interchangeably. Other
currencies were then backed by Pound reserves. Thus,
Pounds and Dollars were the keys to the global financial
system. After the Second World War, the Bretton Woods

agreement created a system with the Dollar pegged to gold at $35 per ounce. Other currencies' exchange rates were set against the Dollar. The high demand for Dollars in post-war Europe and Asia led to the Dollar value increasing relative to other currencies. But by the 1970s, rising US debt led to monetary expansion (more money printing), so that when the 1973 Oil Crisis arrived, inflation rose dramatically and threatened the gold standard. Then there was a second Bretton Woods agreement to have free-floating currencies, so governments could set their values against each other freely. We therefore now had a global market where countries could secretly or openly increase or decrease their currencies' values against the USD or other currencies. China is the most notable example of a country taking advantage of this opportunity by keeping its currency weak against the USD so they could be very competitive in exports to the US – thus exporting more to the US than importing from the US. US Dollars to pay for those exports then flowed to China, increasing its foreign reserves. Chinese exports ballooned and the US suffered an enormous trade deficit with China.

The Universe of Cryptocurrencies

Underlying the difficulty of gauging money supply is the rise of cryptocurrencies. Cryptocurrencies exist as digital messages that their purveyors hope will become a

medium of exchange just like other currencies. The idea
is to use powerful cryptography to ensure safe financial
transactions. What is different from traditional currencies, in addition to its existence as an electric charge, is
that there is decentralized control with no single money
controller or central banking system. The question, of
course, is how such a decentralized system can be developed and maintained. This has been done through what
is called a blockchain, where a number of participants are
linked in an electronic chain with each participant being
a "block" in the chain and where each and every
transaction made by any participant is shared by all other
members of the chain. This becomes a public financial
transaction database designed to assure transparency and
security. All members of the chain have access to the
ledger. Although Bitcoin was the first open-source
software issued in 2009, it was estimated that, as of
2019, there were at least 4,000 cryptocurrencies.

Under normal currency systems, a central bank
controls the supply; but in the cryptocurrency arena,
individuals or companies can produce new units by
various solutions to complex mathematical problems that
only large computer power can complete. In most of the
cryptocurrencies, there is an apparent limit on the total
amount of the currency to be put in circulation, so the
lure of shortages and thus higher prices is an important
element in the attraction to the unit. Of course, no one
really knows what is out there.

The origin of Bitcoin, the first well known crypto-currency, can be traced to October 2008, just as the rest of the economic world was reeling from the collapse of the investment bank Lehman Brothers and the subsequent threat to the financial world. At that time, a white paper was posted on a cryptography message board by a mysterious "Satoshi Nakamoto" who no one had ever seen or ever met. *"I've been working on a new electronic cash system that's fully peer-to-peer, with no trusted party,"* he wrote. Nakamoto described the main properties of his system as follows: *"Double spending is prevented with a peer-to-peer network. No mint or other trusted parties. Participants can be anonymous. New coins are made from 'Hashcash' style proof-of-work. The proof-of-work for new coin generation also powers the network to prevent double-spending."* The nine-page paper, entitled simply "Bitcoin: A Peer-to-Peer Electronic Cash System," concluded with notes on the scheme's purported strengths, giving the following incredible statement: *"We have proposed a system for electronic transactions without relying on trust."*

That sense of attempting to create something different is still apparent on Bitcoin's main webpage today: it proclaims itself as a new kind of money at the top of its homepage. It proceeds to boast that *"Bitcoin uses peer-to-peer technology to operate with no central authority or banks; managing transactions and the issuing of Bitcoins is carried out collectively by the network."* On its webpage listing its innovative elements, Bitcoin claims that it *"offers solutions to many of the trust problems that plague banks. With selective accounting transparency, digital contracts and irreversible transactions, Bitcoin can be used as a ground to restore trust and agreement. Crooked banks cannot cheat the system to make a profit at the expense of other banks or the public. A future in which major banks would support Bitcoin could help to reinstate integrity and trust in financial situations."* The paper failed to point out that faith in the encryption was necessary!

The Bitcoin system has been described as a combination of encryption and peer-to-peer networking where, rather than a physical asset, owners have a digital key, like a password, to a certain amount of Bitcoin. Each Bitcoin is timestamped at the time of its creation and contains a blockchain record of everyone who has owned it in order to avoid fraud and fake Bitcoins. The peer-to-peer networking results in a decentralized system that its proponents say is all but impossible for hackers to attack. In the Bitcoin system, the total amount of Bitcoin available was supposedly fixed by the source code at a maximum of 21 million Bitcoins. New Bitcoins were produced by "miners" who were rewarded with Bitcoin by solving a complex computing problem by a combination of processing power and luck. The number of "miners" increasing the need for more computer power and electric power to run the computers led to interesting cases where, for example, Bitcoin miners in Venezuela used too much electricity and caused blackouts. The fact that cryptocurrencies like Bitcoin were continuously being created meant that the money supply was increasing on a global scale.

There also could be some unusual losses. In one 2018 report, a computer owner threw away an old computer hard drive because he had spilled lemonade on it. But the hard drive had the key for 7,500 Bitcoins, worth a possible $75 million. He tried to convince the local government officials in charge of the landfill to help recover the hard drive. Apparently, this case was not unique. As of 2018, it was estimated that as many as three million Bitcoins were missing as a result of such problems. It is unknown as to what would happen to the supply and prices if those Bitcoins were recovered!

If we can say that it is still "too soon to tell" about managing paper money after seven hundred years, a single decade is surely too short to judge whether Bitcoin is the future of money, or merely a Ponzi scheme for the digital age. One thing is clear, the prices of Bitcoin and other cryptocurrencies have experienced very high volatility, creating fortunes and losing fortunes for those who participate in buying and selling them.

Probably the most important aspect of the cryptocurrency developments is how it promised to screw up any calculations of the money supply. In 2018, the market capitalization of all cryptocurrencies stood at around $417 billion, according to data from industry website CoinMarketCap. The organization of all central bankers, the Bank for International Settlements, estimated in 2018 that the total amount of money in the world was about $5 trillion. According to the CIA, the total amount was $80 trillion if "broad money" was included. So, the $417 billion of cryptocurrencies was significant, but not overwhelmingly so. The reality is that no one really knows what is already out there and what will be created going forward.

Summary

The elastic and expanding supply of paper money always bears the risk of economic instability and rising prices. Some economists even claim that inflation is <u>always</u> a monetary phenomenon: An increasing supply of money leads to the deterioration of the value attributed to a currency, and to the loss of its credibility. Sellers of goods and services will demand more and more of that currency, prices will rise and buyers' purchasing power will diminish. This, in turn, will create discontent among voters and, in the worst case, end in hyperinflation.

6 Measuring Inflation

As there are wide disagreements among economists as to inflation's root cause, it is perhaps not surprising that the inflation figures themselves are also a source of argument. Although the CPI – the Consumer Price Index – is the most commonly used measure, there exists an alphabet soup of inflation indicators in addition to the CPI such as the Personal Consumption Expenditures Price Index (PCEPI), the Employment Cost Index (ECI), the Producer Price Index (PPI), the Harmonized Index for Consumer Prices (HICP), and others.

Why You Can't Trust the Inflation Numbers

In a January 2011 *Wall Street Journal* online article by Brett Arends, the headline read: "Why You Can't Trust the Inflation Numbers." Arends said people on Wall

Street did not worry about inflation since in the previous
12 months the CPI had risen by only 1.5% – a very low
rate. And if the volatile food and energy costs were
stripped out, then the rate was a meager 0.8%. Many
economists were pointing out that wages were rising by
less than 2% a year. With so many people still out of
work, went the line, labor costs were going to stay low
for a long time too. Investors holding inflation-protected
bonds which had fallen in price with the low inflation
rate were losing. He said that ten-year Treasury bonds
yielded less than they did when President Eisenhower left
office. But he warned there was a lot to worry about
because the inflation numbers could not be trusted. Over
the previous 30 years, the federal government under
every government of both Republican and Democratic
parties had made changes in the way inflation was calculated and the changes tended to flatten the inflation rate.

Arends pointed to findings by John Williams at
Shadow Government Statistics who had said that if
inflation was still calculated with the same set of items,
the inflation numbers came out lower because of
replacement. If the price of steak rose, the government
assumed consumers purchased cheaper hamburger, so
they replaced steak with hamburger. It thus looked like
the price went down. The price of a Mac computer was
reduced because of technical improvements using
"hedonics." Hedonics is an effort to adjust inflation to

take account for product quality changes. So a product may have increased in price, but the price increase was due to improved quality and not inflation. If a computer increased in price by 10% and the computer was exactly the same, then it would reflect an inflation of 10%; but if the speed and efficiency of the computer was improved by the manufacturer, the price increase could not be considered inflationary since, in essence, the actual product has changed and a comparison was not possible.

Another reason for not trusting the statistics was that they were backward-looking and registered what had happened, not what was about to happen. At the time of Arends' article, the United Nations Food Price Index had just hit a new record high and oil prices had reached nearly $90 a barrel. These raw material price rises were not yet reflected in the consumer price index and supermarket prices of the coming months. He also said that the inflation figures could not be trusted because the Federal Reserve had been flooding the world with extra dollars, doubling the size of the monetary base in order to keep the American economy from crashing.

The History of Measuring Inflation

Apparently, the earliest study of index numbers was formulated in 1704 by Bishop William Fleetwood in

England who published *Chronicon Preciosum: Or An Account of English Money, the Price of Corn and Other Commodities for the Last 600 Years*. The reason he made this study was that an Oxford college required members to swear to vacate their position if their personal estate income was more than 5 British Pounds per annum. That requirement was written in the 1400s and the question was whether, in the year 1700, a student or teacher might conscientiously take this oath even if he possessed a larger estate income since the value of money had fallen during those 300 years. Fleetwood, therefore, did a comparison of prices between 1400 and 1700 in British Pounds Sterling of four commodities: corn, meat, beverages, and cloth. He concluded that the present value of those commodities was about 25 Pounds. He therefore said that a member who had an income of 30 Pounds or less should be considered to have the same income as 5 Pounds in the 1400s.

In line with trying to make inflation adjustments, in 1780, the state of Massachusetts government issued bonds with a value indexed to a "Tabular Standard" in order to stop unrest among soldiers fighting in the war for independence who were being paid in those bonds and who were afraid that their value would decline because of rising prices.

More modern definitions of inflation can be traced back to the economist Irving Fisher who studied the subject at the end of the nineteenth century. According to Zachary Karabell in his book *The Leading Indicators,* Fisher was *"... a minister's son imbued with a firm sense of right and wrong and a background in mathematics."* He believed that *"economic patterns could be observed and quantified as scientific phenomena."* Working with Wesley Mitchell, an undergraduate at the University of Chicago, they created the essentials of price indexes as we know them today. Fisher's dissertation was on *Mathematical Investigations in the Theory of Value and Prices,* which he then used as the basis for the undergraduate classes he taught. Fisher was unhappy with the work of the Bureau of Labor Statistics (BLS) which had been founded as part of the the Department of the Interior in 1884, to collect information about employment and labor. The BLS had started the Consumer Price Index statistic in 1919. In the 1920s Fisher set up the Index Number Institute, to see if he could do better.

Mitchell and Fisher faced the challenge of how to gather the information and adjust for changes in consumer tastes and habits in different parts of the country. Then there was the challenge of which items on the list representing the "basket" of goods and services consumed by people. Rather than consumers purchasing the same 100 goods over time, tastes changed. Fisher's answer to this was to change the weights of the various goods and services.

The prices included in the basket and the significance of the different price changes depended on how much of the various goods and services households bought. A product or service that was consumed on a large scale was given greater weight than one that was consumed on a lesser scale. This meant that price changes on a product or service that were consumed on a large scale had a greater impact on the CPI than price changes on a product or service consumed on a lesser scale.

Having worked out what should be in the basket of goods to accurately reflect consumer behavior, the second step was to calculate the value of that basket regularly, on a monthly basis. The Index altered each month based on the changes in the prices of the representative items. If the value of all the index items increases by 10%, then the inflation rate will be 10%. The basic fault of the system was the changing components of the index, with index components being changed on the basis of consumer surveys – which themselves were subject to error.

Building the Index

As of the early 2000s, the US used a CPI measurement system which started with the construction of a "market basket" of goods and services for the "typical" consumer in the economy. The research included thousands of items divided into hundreds of categories of consumer products or services under major groups: food, housing, apparel, transportation, medical care, recreation, education and communication, and "other." The basket of items would be adjusted every few years according to changes in the purchasing patterns of families.

The Bureau of Labor Statistics researchers interviewed families all over America to find out what the families actually purchased, so the specific items purchased the most could be included in the Index. In addition to the survey, families were asked to keep diaries of their spending habits. The prices included in the basket and the significance of the different price changes depended on how much of the various goods and services house-holds bought. A product or service that was consumed on a large scale was given greater weight than one that was consumed on a lesser scale. This meant that price changes on a product or service that was consumed on a large scale had a greater impact on the CPI than price changes on a product or service consumed on a lesser scale. The next step in the process was to determine the price of each item in the basket regularly, mostly monthly, and then calculate the value of the entire basket – of course taking into account the different weights of each good and service. If the value of the entire basket rose by 10% then the CPI inflation rate would be 10%.

Each Index had to have a "baseline" date against which subsequent data was measured. In the US, the CPI was based on price levels in the 1980s so that the baseline was set at 100. In the early 2000s, according to the *Handbook of Methods Bureau of Labor Statistics,* each month, the US Bureau of Labor Statistics (BLS) collected about 70,000 prices from about 21,000 outlets in 88 regions around the country. These 88 regions were known as Primary Sampling Units (PSU). In five large urban areas, including eight PSUs, prices were collected each month for all items, while in the other regions, prices of only food, fuels, and a few other items were collected. Prices for other items were collected bimonthly. In addition, information from approximately 40,000 rental tenants or landlords and about 20,000 homeowners was collected for the housing portion of the CPI. For gasoline prices, the prices from individual filling stations in the New York area would be aggregated to create an index of gasoline prices in that area. The same would be done for all other price groups, such as new automobiles, doctor's services, women's dresses, ground beef, etc. Some of these groups were homogeneous, but others were not. For example, you might say that ground beef is pretty much the same all over but, of course, that is open to debate. In some cases, such as doctor's services, the range of possibilities is wide. Nevertheless, all the various items on the list were assumed to give full coverage of all consumer expenditures. But already biases had crept in. For example, medical care costs only included those paid out of pocket or that part not covered by health insurance.

Gin and Inflation Measurement

The history of gin gives us some insight into how measures of inflation confront enormous challenges. In March 2017, the Office for National Statistics (ONS) in the UK announced that the popular alcoholic drink gin would be one of the new items added into the basket of goods whose prices the ONS used to measure inflation. It was the first time that gin had been included specifically in the basket of goods since 2004. Prior to that, the price of gin had been included in the 1950s, first as part of "spirits" and then in its own right; it then slipped out of the category of "wine and spirits."

In 2015, sales of gin overtook whisky in the UK; in 2016, it enjoyed record sales of over £1 billion. In 2017, 40 million bottles were sold in the UK, enough to make 1.12 billion gin and tonics, or 28 for every adult in the country. At that time, gin was not only big business but came in an ever-increasing variety of flavors – citrus, coriander, and cardamom are just some of the ingredients added into high-end boutique brands that led to commentators talking of a gin "renaissance." Because of its revived popularity, the ONS added it to the basket of goods in March 2017.

But gin wasn't the only item returning to the basket. After a similar length of absence, bicycle helmets were also re-introduced – a reflection of the growth in the sport and recreational cycling following British success both at the Olympics and the Tour de France. Other items that were new in the 2017 basket included half chocolate-coated biscuits, non-dairy milk, flavored water, cough liquid, children's scooters, and jigsaws. Items taken out of the basket included menthol cigarettes, single drainer sinks, motor vehicle brake pads, mobile phone handsets, and a child's swing.

Over the years, the basket of goods has created a fascinating snapshot of how consumer spending habits have changed and how society has changed and evolved. The entries in the 1947 UK basket included rabbit, cooking fat, boiled sweets, tweed sports coats, corsets, rubber roller table mangles, and cod liver oil. The 1970 list of items included cream crackers, five different types of bacon (middle, back, streaky, collar, and gammon), a keg of stout, latex-backed carpets, ethylene slacks, a woman's shampoo and set, and football match tickets.

It might be fascinating stuff, but the ONS in the UK and the equivalent government organizations in other countries weren't just compiling these lists to look at how society was changing for the sake of it. The purpose of creating, compiling, and updating the basket of goods was in order to accurately monitor the rate of price changes in the economy. But it's a challenge that has been more difficult than it might first appear – and one that when the results are wrong could have serious and ongoing implications.

The Boskin Commission

In 1995, the US Senate formed an "Advisory Commission to Study the Consumer Price Index" headed by Stanford University professor Michael Boskin. The objective was to study the possible bias in how the Consumer Prices Index (CPI) was calculated by the US Bureau of Labor Statistics. There was a suspicion that the statistics overstated inflation and this had an important impact on government policy. The Boskin Commission reported in late 1996 that the CPI overstated inflation by about 1.1% per year in 1996 and about 1.3% prior to 1996. If the 1.3% is compounded over a ten-year period, the error was substantial. The political aspect of this effort was important because the Index was used to calculate the annual payment increases in various retirement and compensation programs, the most important one being government Social Security payments. The findings indicated that the US government expenditures on retirement programs had increased more than they should have. More importantly, future budget deficit projections were too large. The conclusion was that the overstatement of inflation would add $691 billion to the national debt by 2006.

In 1997, Allan Greenspan, the US Federal Reserve chairman, confirmed that the Consumer Price Index overstated inflation by between 0.5 and 1.5 percentage points a year and he called on Congress to make changes.

Mr Greenspan said Fed economists' research essentially confirmed the findings of the Boskin Commission and concluded that the overstatement would result in $148 billion in overpayments to recipients of Social Security and federal benefit programs by the year 2006 unless changes were made.

The Boskin report said that there were four main sources of bias in inflation statistics:

1. Substitution Bias,
2. Outlet Substitution Bias,
3. Quality Change Bias, and
4. New Product Bias.

Substitution Bias, the report said, occurred when there were price changes and consumers substituted less expensive products for more expensive ones. *Outlet Substitution Bias* occurred when consumers went to lower price retail outlets that were not originally in the retail sample used by the data gatherers. *Quality Change Bias* took place when products had quality improvements, such as better energy efficiency or more durability, that was not measured. *New Product Bias* occurred when new products were not included in the market basket or were included only after a long time lag. All these biases rendered the CPI inaccurate, the report said. These biases succinctly stated the key problems with inflation measurements.

The key challenge in constructing inflation indices is that we're living in a world of rapid economic change and it's hard to define exactly what is meant by the cost of living when new goods are being introduced on a daily basis. It may be easy to measure the change in the price of a bottle of milk, but how can change be calculated when a new drug that cures cancer is found when cancer was untreatable before? More and more people are purchasing goods that did not exist previously.

The problem of quality is also a significant challenge. There are a number of goods that are ostensibly the same today as they were before, but which have changed dramatically over the years. One example of that would be the automobile. Today's automobiles are very different and much improved than in the past, now offering all kinds of conveniences that did not exist before.

The introduction of budget airlines has now made air travel much cheaper than it was previously, an example of substitution bias. The product is exactly the same, but the lower-priced product has been substituted and may be overlooked by the data gatherers. The result is an excessive increase in the CPI not warranted by what is actually happening in the market.

Outlet substitution bias can result if new outlets are included in the sample of retail outlets used by the index price data gatherers. One outlet could have a lower or higher price than another outlet, and selection of the

wrong outlet could have an impact on the index numbers. Now, with internet shopping, the challenge is
increasing since only relying on physical retail outlets
may overstate substantially what the prices of goods and
services are since, as everyone knows, internet prices are
often much cheaper than what the physical retail outlets
charge. Amazon prices have illustrated this time and time
again. The type of delivery is also critical. Purchasing a
physical book is normally much more expensive than
having it transmitted electronically so it can be read on
an iPad. But the biggest effect came because the CPI
underestimated the benefits shoppers gain from improvements in product quality and from the plethora of new
products.

US GDP Numbers Questioned

In 2013, the investor Peter Schiff argued that for many
years, official government figures were suggesting that
the US economy was much larger than it actually was.
This, he said, was due to the way that the country's Gross
Domestic Product (GDP) was calculated. When producing the figures, the government came up with two categories: "nominal" GDP, which didn't take inflation into
account; and "real" GDP, in which the figure was
adjusted to take price rises into account. To get to the
second more widely used figure, rather than using the

CPI, which was produced by the Bureau of Labor Statistics, a second measurement called the GDP Deflator, compiled by the Bureau of Economic Analysis, was used. This measurement differed from the CPI by having greater flexibility in how it weighed and chose the goods and services included in its sample basket. Between 1947 and 1977, the figures produced by the Bureau of Labor Statistics and by the Bureau of Economic Analysis were almost identical, both rising 173% for that 30-year period. After that, however, the two sets of figures diverged: between 1977 and 2013, the CPI rose almost three times, at 292%; by contrast, the GDP Deflator figures showed a rise of just over double, at 209%.

According to Schiff, the official government figures, using the GDP Deflator, put the US economy at about $17 trillion. But swapping the GDP Deflator for the CPI over that 36-year period resulted in the US economy looking substantially smaller, at $13 trillion. In other words, the economy was 28% smaller than believed. This example illustrates vividly how depending on the choice and weight of products measured by an index inflation numbers could vary enormously.

What Are People REALLY Buying?

In UK opinion polling, there has long been a phenomenon called "Shy Tories." This is where, when people are asked the way they will vote in a general election, some do not tell the pollster their true intentions, through not wanting to be embarrassed or not wanting the pollster to think badly of them. The Shy Tory phenomenon has been used to explain the occasions when the opinion polls called the general election wrong, as happened in 1969, 1992, and 2015. It's something that is not unique to the UK; in the US, a similar trend is known as the Bradley Effect, after pollsters in California wrongly predicted Tom Bradley would win the 1982 race for governor. More recently, Shy Trump voters might also have led to the surprise result of the 2016 presidential election. Given the way Trump was being lambasted and pilloried in the popular press, many people didn't want to admit that they liked him or would vote for him.

Any survey is only as good as the information given by the people taking the questionnaire, and that is true in all sorts of areas. One of the problems for the health services in dealing with the effects of alcohol, for example, is that people underestimate how much they are consuming. Similarly, people can be exceedingly modest about how much they access adult porn sites on the internet; in January 2017, the website Pornhub revealed that 92 billion videos had been watched on its site over the previous 12 months: in viewing time that constituted 6 billion hours, or 524,641 years. These are huge numbers, yet are never reflected in official surveys of consumer use.

Of course, Pornhub is one of many other porn sites so the numbers and hours are probably substantially higher.

In a similar way, the "market basket" formulation of inflation is subject to many possible errors because it is based on what people "say" they buy, and that may not correspond with what they actually buy. For example, work by the Office of National Statistics in 2014 suggested that the use of banned drugs and prostitution in the UK was worth close to £11 billion (£4.3 billion for prostitution and £6.7 billion for drugs). By adding these figures into the overall GDP, it meant that the UK overtook France to become the world's fifth-largest consumer of prostitution services and illicit drugs. But while substantial amounts of money are clearly spent on these products, survey respondents are extremely unlikely to reveal their own individual usage.

The Changing Time and Place Bias

The result is that the official inflation figures are skewed away from how people are actually spending their money. The figures are also affected by the fact that the times between updating the market basket list may be too long, particularly in view of the speed at which new products and services are being offered. Finally, the inflation researchers do not revise the index backward in time when updating the market basket, so, in essence, they are comparing apples and oranges.

In the US, two sources were used to obtain quantitative data. The Census Bureau conducted a "Point of Purchase Survey" (POPS), which was a survey of households to identify the distribution of household expenditures in various outlets. Then the BLS, on the basis of that data, selected a sample of outlets according to the outlets' shares in total expenditures in the particular survey area for a particular item. After the outlet's sample was determined, the BLS researchers visited each selected outlet and choose one or more specific items (such as a particular brand of soap powder) to be priced. Any specific item's chance of being selected was based on its share of the outlet's revenue, so the more popular items would have a better chance of being selected. The procedure of outlet and item selection was part of the sample rotation process which periodically refreshed the sample.

Although the BLS tried to reprice exactly the same items from month to month, it was often not possible either because a previously priced item had sold out, or was discontinued or unavailable for one reason or another. This could happen quite frequently, particularly when it came to women's clothing with its frequent style changes. Imagine trying to find the same item in the "fast fashion" stores of H&M, Forever 21, or Zara. When an item was not found, a new one was substituted by a BLS researcher. The BLS had a set of guidelines that should be used to find direct comparisons. Then, if a direct comparison couldn't be found, a new item was used with the price adjusted accordingly. But both of these decisions were highly subjective ones, taken by the particular researcher.

Market-Basket Bias

The "market basket" formation is subject to many possible errors not just because the selection of items may be wrong, but because they are based on what people "say" they buy and that may not correspond with what they actually buy. For example, we know that sales of illegal drugs are enormous, but it would be unusual for a survey respondent to admit that a substantial portion of his or her budget went on drug purchases.

Then, of course, is the question of how to decide how much an average consumer spends. Second, how does taxation figure into the total income available to a particular family? What is the cost of living after that? Then, as regards medical care, how much is paid from insurance and how much comes out of the pocket of the consumer? People receiving social security and pensions have different financial situations from people who don't.

Then there is the issue of maintaining a representative CPI sample of goods and services. This is next to impossible given the constantly changing list of new items being offered to consumers. In addition, there are some sales outlets closing and others opening. So there needs to be a refreshment of these in order to be representative.

Then there are the problems of quality changes in individual items. As prices change, consumers may tend to minimize costs by changing the purchasing mix and there will be a tendency to buy more of products whose prices have declined and less of those whose prices have risen.

Data Gathering Difficulties

In 2005, some critics questioned the accuracy of government inflation numbers as regards to hotel prices. In my travels, I've seen tremendous changes in hotel room rates. In the 1970s, I was able to get a good hotel room for $100 per night, but by the year 2000, the same room would cost closer to $300 per night. In 2005, according to the Labor Department, hotel prices were down 2.5% in September from a year earlier, but industry executives said that prices were actually rising significantly. One statistician said that the government's index of hotel prices didn't include the price of hotels for business travel and that tended to strip out higher price business rates. Hotel operators like Hilton, Marriott, Starwood, and others were reporting double-digit growth in revenues per available room, a sign that increases in nightly rates were taking place.

Complexity

The complexity of measuring consumer prices is illustrated by one section of a 2015 paper in the UK, discussing the methodology used by the Office for National Statistics (ONS):

> *Consumer price indices can measure the costs of consumption at three main points; at the point that goods and services are acquired, when payments for these goods and services are made, and when they are used. For some goods and services, the three are close to each other. For longer-lasting goods such as furniture, household appliances and cars (called durable goods), the price to acquire the product can be different to the amount it would cost to use such an item over the same period of time if, for example, one might hire the item. However, most statisticians agree that such items can be treated in the same way as non-durable goods and services. Property is the main exception to this rule. The rate at which a property declines in value, or depreciates, is much slower than most other durable goods. Property can retain or even increase its value over time if properly maintained. The*

acquisition, payment, and use of owner-occupier housing costs requires different leads to different estimates. Other goods that appreciate over time, such as antiques, are usually not included in consumer price statistics.[54]

Data Gathering

The difficulty and complexity of gathering price information is mind-bending when we look at just a sampling of the items being collected in surveys:

Passenger transport by railway.

Passenger transport by road.

Passenger transport by air.

Passenger transport by sea and inland waterway.

Postal services.

Telephone and telefax equipment and services.

Audio-visual equipment and related products.

Reception and reproduction of sound and pictures.

Photographic, cinematographic, and optical equipment.

Data processing equipment.

Recording media.

Repair of audio-visual equipment and related products.

Other major durables for recreation and culture.

Major durables for in/outdoor recreation.

Other recreational items, gardens, and pets.

Games, toys, and hobbies.

Equipment for sport and open-air recreation.

Gardens, plants, and flowers.

Pets, related products, and services.

Recreational and cultural services.

Recreational and sporting services.

Cultural services.

Books, newspapers, and stationery.

Miscellaneous printed matter, stationery, drawing materials.

Package holidays.

Education.

Catering services.

Restaurants and cafés.

Canteens.

Accommodation services.

Personal care.

Hairdressing and personal grooming establishments.

Appliances and products for personal care.

Personal effects.

Jewelry, clocks, and watches.

Other personal effects.

Social protection.

Insurance.

House contents insurance.

Health insurance.

Transport insurance.

Financial services.

Urban–Rural Inflation Differences In China

In September of 2004, in an interview published in the
OECD Observer, Enrico Giovannini, the OECD's chief
statistician, gave an unofficial view on the value of statistics following the Boskin Report's criticisms of the inflation statistics in the US. When Giovannini was director
for economic statistics at the Italian Statistical Institute,
they decided to update the Consumer Price Index
categories yearly. Comparing the official inflation numbers with perceived inflation as measured by opinion
surveys, before the introduction of the euro in 2002, the
two lines were in synch. But after the euro introduction,
perceived inflation rose more steeply than the official
measure. Apparently, with the euro introduction, some
prices of frequently bought items rose more than others.
It was difficult to assign the correct value to the new

notes and coins, so shoppers could have overestimated the value of the new currency.

Currency Confusion – The Tenge

In 1993, Kazakhstan issued a new Tenge currency in the hope that it would end an inflationary spiral that was taking place. The new currency replaced the old Ruble banknotes which had circulated since Soviet days. There was a great deal of confusion as street traders tried to convert inflated Rubles into Tenge before realizing that nobody wanted to buy the Ruble. At the time, the inflation numbers were shown to average 30% a month in the first ten months of 1993 and the government was panicking. They were concerned that they were on the edge of hyperinflation. But of course, the confusion regarding which currency to use muddied the water considerably. Eventually the Ruble disappeared, the Tenge became the main currency and with the economy picking up in the late 1990s inflation stabilized.

Pakistan Statistics Concerns

In 2012, Pakistan's Bureau of Statistics' method of calculating the Consumer Price Index was called into question. When announcing the numbers for March of that year at a 10.8% rise, the statistics secretary said that the 38% rise in electricity prices during the month had not been incorporated because of "technical reasons." He explained that there was a retroactive increase in electricity prices announced in August 2011, but charged in March of 2012. That logic did not satisfy consumers who suffered an increase in their electricity bills. Another dispute centered around the 15.4% drop in the price of milk solely on the basis of one cantonment board's decision to freeze prices in their area – which did not apply to the rest of the country. Critics pointed to the fact that the Bureau of Statistics was not fully independent and thus was influenced by the government's political agenda. The International Food Policy Research Institute (IFPRI), a Washington-based research organization, said that the CPI computation in Pakistan primarily depicted inflation in urban areas only and overlooked rural settlements. They also mentioned the problems in the weighting of various commodity categories in the Pakistan Index. Critics said that the government was manipulating the statistics by changing the weightings of the Index components to show a reduction in inflation.

China's Suspect Statistics

In 1995, reports surfaced that China's inflation statistics were unreliable, thus making it difficult for organizations such as the United Nations, International Monetary

Fund, and World Bank to estimate how big the economy was.

At that time, China adjusted the contents of the basket of goods and services in its Index in order to keep up with the fast-changing economy. The Index was based on household spending surveys from detailed records kept by thousands of families across the country.

The basis of doubt stemmed from the Great Leap Forward time in the late 1950s when false grain production statistics were published despite a terrible famine which led to the deaths of as many as 30 million Chinese. After that, the Chinese government stopped publishing statistics until the 1970s. There was a continuing concern that production numbers were inflated. A number of state-owned companies' performances were based on output instead of profit. So, it is not surprising that the government statistical bureau uncovered thousands of cases of statistics fraud. When Jiangsu province reported unusually high numbers, the bureau auditors found that the poorer inland townships were reporting inflated numbers.

In February 2011, China's inflation statistics were being questioned. An overhaul of the country's main inflation measurement had exposed some long-standing problems. Some critics said the government was intentionally misleading the public, but others said that the government had simply been too slow in keeping up with changes impacting the economy, so the economic picture was not an accurate one. The government announced a high increase in the share of housing costs in the consumer goods basket measuring inflation and reduced the weights in a number of other items. But some critics said that non-food price inflation was underestimated not because of the weighting, but because actual prices were not being reflected in the CPI. The official data showed that consumer prices in January had risen by 4.9%, but independent economists estimated 5.3%. Analysts worried that the agency had not made adjustments fast and far enough. For example, the statistics agency used mortgage rates to estimate changes in residential rents, but since housing prices had soared in recent years while borrowing costs stayed flat, housing costs were being grossly underestimated. Interestingly, the Chinese statistics agency had acknowledged that shortcoming and said that it would be fixed, but had been slow in implementing this. There were also disputes about clothing prices which independent analysts had said were too low since prices had risen faster than the government had estimated.

In 2011, Reuters reported that Chinese statisticians were struggling to keep pace with the economy and the new CPI placed more weight on underestimated prices. They said the lack of transparency hurt the credibility of the Chinese data. They reported that the government had been far too slow to keep up with changes sweeping the economy and therefore was not painting an accurate picture of the reality on the ground. One economist said that non-food price inflation was underestimated because actual prices were not being reflected in the Consumer Price Index.

One said that by placing extra emphasis on housing, the CPI basket now gave prominence to a deeply flawed set of price data that would make reported inflation too low.

UK Inflation Index Credibility

In the UK in August 2006, there was controversy surrounding the Consumer Price Index when the Office for National Statistics (ONS) said that its measured inflation fell the previous month despite the fact that the electricity and gas prices rose at the fastest rate in over 26 years.

Edmund Conway, writing in the *Daily Telegraph,* commented that the ONS was understating the effect of higher utility bills on the overall inflation number, saying that the weighting of gas bills in the inflation calculations had risen only by 17% while the actual cost of gas had gone up by 64%. He said that this discrepancy necessitated a revision of how much weighting was given to each component of the CPI. Some experts warned that the official inflation measures hid the fact that pensioners' cost of living was rising faster than other members of the population.

In 2008, research by the *Daily Telegraph* indicated that the rising food and fuel prices, as well as increased taxes and other household bills, suggested that the average family was experiencing inflation that was twice as high as official estimates. According to their Real Cost of Living Index gathered with moneysupermarket.com, a price comparison website, prices were rising by 9.5% while the government CPI was only 3%. They said that one explanation was that the CPI did not include council tax or mortgage costs which were important expenditures for many families. They said that tax was very important in calculating inflation, since income tax and national insurance contributions absorbed 36% of the average family's income. They said that grocery bills had risen by an average of 23% over the previous year, but the prices of individual items had risen to a much greater extent – such as rice which had gone up by 80% and frozen peas up by 73%. They also said that because bank interest rates on mortgages had risen despite falling house prices, there had been an increase of 11% in weekly mortgage costs.

Examining interest rates, they said that although the Bank of England had held the base rate at 5% since April, as far as the consumer was concerned, interest rates continued to rise with banks, giving a shock to those coming to the end of their fixed-rate mortgage term. And although house prices had been falling, there had been an 11% increase in weekly mortgage costs.

India – Data Gathering Difficulties

In 2005, the Ministry of Commerce and Industry in India made revisions in the wholesale price index list of products. The number of items was markedly different between 1970–71 and 2004–5. The number of primary articles such as food and minerals rose from 80 to 102, fuel and power commodities rose from 10 to 19, manufactured products increased from 270 to 555, so overall the number of products in the index rose from 360 to 676. At the same time, the number of price quotations gathered increased from 1,295 for the 1970–71 series to 5,492 for 2004–05. The obvious question, therefore, was how these two sets of numbers could be reasonably compared.

The Brazil Experience

Brazil has had a lot of experience with inflation; in fact, hyperinflation. In April of 1990, inflation indices were at an all-time high of 6,821%. I remember arriving at Rio de Janeiro when inflation was down to 2,000% and remarking to my Brazilian friend: *"Wow 2,000% inflation!"* He said: *"Isn't it wonderful? Last week it was 3,000%!"* The Brazilians have therefore become very interested in inflation and how it can be measured. As of early 2000, there were a number of organizations calculating a CPI and other indices. The three most important organizations were

the IBRE FGV (Instituto Brasileiro de Economia linked to
the FGV or Fundação Getúlio Vargas), the IBGE (Instituto
Brasileiro de Geografia e Estatística), and a bureau created
by the São Paulo Municipality.

The FGV produced the IGP-DI (General Price Index)
which was used to correct certain regulated prices and was
at one time used to adjust telecommunications prices.
The IGP-M (General Price Index-Market) was widely
used to adjust financial transactions such as contracts and
inflation-linked treasury bonds, as well as to adjust electricity prices. The FGV also produced the IPA (Broad
Producer Price Index), the IPC (Consumer Price Index),
and the INCC (the National Index of Construction
Costs). Their indices covered the seven largest metropoli-
tan regions in Brazil. In addition, there were a number of
other indices produced by various organizations.

Needless to say, given the different methodologies
used in the various indices, there were significant differences in their movements. Efforts by the government
over many years to restrain inflation resulted in a number
of "plans": the Summer Plan, Collor Plan, Collor II Plan,
and the Real Plan. Each plan required inflation measures
and, given the failure of each one except for the Real
Plan (named after the new currency, the Real), there were
always efforts to change the inflation measures. Also
complicating the process were the frequent currency
changes taking place in Brazil. Between 1967 and 2000,

there were eight currency changes in Brazil – Cruzeiro: used from 1942–67; Cruzeiro Novo (new Cruzeiro): 1967–70; Cruzeiro: used again from 1970–86; Cruzado: from 1986–89; Cruzado Novo: 1989–90; Cruzeiro: used yet again from 1990–93; Cruzeiro Real: used from 1993–94; and the Real introduced in 1994.

In 1986, when the Cruzado Plan was announced in Brazil and the government introduced a major price freeze, people went to the shops to check prices and prevent any rises; but by the time the fourth price freeze was announced by President Collor, no one believed that prices would really stay frozen. One 55-year-old carpenter said to Reuters: *Forget this talk about a freeze. The prices have already gone up during the night. I've seen them go up.* In this kind of environment, it was impossible to keep tabs on where the price in any inflation index would be.

Urban–Rural Inflation Differences In China

The difficult task of aligning different groups even within one country on a single inflation measure was illustrated in a 2009 study by an economist at the People's Bank of China regarding urban–rural inflation differences. In the study, Zhang Xuechun underlined the apparent duality of the Chinese economy, which was segregated into rural and urban markets causing index differences. He noted that with the transition to a market economy, these differences were being reduced but they still existed. The Chinese National Statistics Bureau calculated a CPI but, before 1978, most of the prices were determined by the government and didn't reflect the market's demand and supply. After that, more and more weight was given to the CPI in making policy decisions. In the early years, the differences were significant but, over time, the differences were reduced. Between 1985 and 2008, the urban CPI was much higher than the rural CPI. Starting in 2001, there was a turning point and the rural CPI was slightly higher than the urban one.

The difference between the two indices could be explained as a result of policy measures, development levels, and the differences in consumption behavior. In the early years, the clothing price index in the urban areas was much higher than the rural areas and the urban housing price was higher. There were other differences caused by the difference in costs of transportation and communication, medical costs, and personal items. Looking at housing, material for building, and decoration accounted for a large portion of the rural residents' components of the rural CPI, while rent was the main force in the urban housing component. One interesting point made in the report was that information in rural areas was not as well developed and that, combined with the lower educational level, rural people were not as well-informed regarding prices as the urban residents.

Also, the scale of retail sales in urban areas was far more than in rural areas, adding to differences.

Inflation Differences Within Turkey

In Turkey, geographical differences were also exhibited. In mid-2018, the Istanbul Chamber of Commerce announced that consumer prices in Istanbul increased by 0.52% in July 2018, compared to 1.27% in June 2018 and 0.20% in July 2017. The report noted that the correlation between official inflation and Istanbul inflation was not particularly great and July was a month in which there could be substantial deviations, although the past two years' figures showed better correlation. When we look at the details, we observe that food inflation change in July in Istanbul was 0.7%, vs. the 1.4% price increase in the Ankara food survey, on top of the massive increase in June.

Malaysia Concerns

In January of 1995, there were concerns raised that the Consumer Price Index in Malaysia understated inflation. Further, some critics said that Asian governments, in general, were doing the same thing since they were adjusting the CPI components once every five or ten years, and thus they did not reflect changing spending patterns and the rapid growth in the region's cities since it was in the cities where inflation tended to be the highest. Thus, the CPI, the most widely cited measures of inflation, was slow to reflect changes in spending patterns and the rapid growth of the region's cities.

Malaysian government officials admitted that inflation was higher in the major cities than elsewhere in the country. One reason for the low CPI figures was because some fast-appreciating items, such as housing, were excluded from the index. Also at that time, the government could control key prices such as rice, cooking oil, fertilizer, and fuel which represented almost 40% of the Index.

South Africans Skeptical Too

A report in 2003 said that South Africans were skeptical of official inflation data. It said South Africans should have been exhilarated by Statistics South Africa's announcement that the official inflation rate for April was nearly two percentage points lower than initially expected. The rate of 8.5% instead of 10.4% was much closer to the targeted inflation rate of between 3% and 6% the Reserve Bank has set itself with the backing of the Treasury.

But for the most part, South Africans dismissed the news with a skeptical shrug of the shoulders even though the downward shift in the inflation curve was expected to prompt the Reserve Bank to lower the official interest rate of 13.5%, and thereby put more money in people's pockets. The primary reason for the lower inflation rate was a mistake Statistics SA made in calculating the Consumer Price Index by using outdated and overstated data for the rental component of its calculations. It was no comfort to Statistics SA that it was not its vigilance, or that of government officials, that led to the detection of the error. It was spotted by a portfolio manager at a private bank, though the Treasury then said it raised concerns about the reliability of the Statistics SA data as far back as the beginning of 2002.

The admission of the error and the revised inflation figures for April and March took place against a background of fierce election skirmishes between President Thabo Mbeki and Tony Leon, leader of the main opposition party, the Democratic Alliance, over whether the government was winning its declared war on poverty. Mr. Mbeki cited a raft of economic figures, including ten years of positive economic growth and gains in the Rand against the Dollar over the previous 18 months. But Mr. Leon cited figures that pointed to rising unemployment, particularly in the black community, and the human and economic costs of the AIDS epidemic sweeping the country. He said that for many, in spite of political freedom, life was worse. The politicians' use of data to support opposing positions was unlikely to have bolstered public confidence in either statistics or statisticians. An economist with the Congress of SA Trade Unions said South Africans often challenged data they disliked instead of dealing with the social issues they reflected. He said that there was a tendency, if not a tradition, among politicians in South Africa to manipulate or even manufacture statistics to advance their ideological beliefs.

The most notorious use of statistics for political ends was committed by the old white-only government when it excluded millions of black South Africans from official data, including information garnered by census enumerators, on the grounds that blacks were the citizens of their allotted tribal homelands and not of South Africa.

Income Differences

The difficulty of finding an average income level is illustrated everywhere in the world. For example, in 2016, Greenwich, Connecticut was the home of a number of wealthy hedge fund managers, making it one of the richest towns of the US. But within Connecticut itself, there were extreme differences between the wealth of Greenwich and cities like Hartford, the state capital. In Bridgeport, an industrial city, up the coast from Greenwich, the high rate of income inequality was even worse. Therefore, trying to arrive at an index that represented all people was an impossible task.

What Statistics Fail to Measure

In March 1968, Robert Kennedy gave a speech to the University of Kansas as part of his campaign to be US president. In it, he was famously critical of how GDP was used as a figure to measure a nation. *"Our Gross National Product, now, is over $800 billion dollars a year,"* he told his audience, *"but that Gross National Product counts air pollution and cigarette advertising, and ambulances to clear our highways of carnage. Yet the gross national product does not allow for the health of our children, the quality of their education or the joy of their play. It does not include the beauty of our poetry or the strength of our marriages, the intelligence of our public debate or the integrity of our public officials. It measures neither our wit nor our courage, neither our wisdom nor our learning, neither our compassion nor our devotion to our country, it measures everything in short, except that which makes life worthwhile."*[55]

Summary

As sophisticated as computer models get, accurately capturing actual human behavior is incredibly difficult. It starts with the complexity of sampling items that represent a "typical" consumer—if such a thing exists—and keeping them aligned with the continuously changing consumer behavior and the release of new and improved products. At the same time, the consequences of a possible erroneous measurement of inflation numbers are enormous: if the inflation figures are wrong, this means that, not only are governments making decisions on the basis of false information, but, as individuals in our daily lives, so are we.

7 Controlling and Manipulating Inflation

Governments' Vested Interest

Revision of the CPI is a political hot potato because the Index is used to calculate payments that matter to tens of millions of people. In the US, the CPI number impacts the size of cost-of-living adjustments for federal benefit programs such as Social Security, civilian and military retirement, welfare for the elderly, and food stamps. Many features of the tax code, such as the size of the personal exemption and the standard deduction, are also indexed to the CPI.

As illustrated by the Boskin Commission report, any decision to change either the CPI itself or the way in which it is used to determine benefit levels and tax liabilities could trim hundreds of billions of dollars from future federal budget deficits, which was why the Boskin Commission was appointed in the first place.

Clearly, then, it is in the vested interest of governments of all stripes to influence inflation figures, whether in terms of attracting foreign loans or investment or in terms of reducing wage demands. And when the government has a hand in how those figures are put together, the temptation to manipulate them is always there. Even when governments are well-behaved and put proper distance between themselves and those compiling the statistics, it is also apparent how easy it is to come up with different inflation figures – and the huge repercussions that even a discrepancy of a fraction of a percentage point can have.

Central Banks Control Attempts

Central banks have been criticized for tightening money supply even when borrowing rates are very low, but then adopting an inflationary fiscal policy when inflation is rising. There is a continuous battle between economists and policymakers regarding the right interpretation of the data and what actions should be taken. There are the liberals who argue that by relaxing fiscal policy, i.e. increase government spending, the economy will grow and debts will be easier to pay. Also, by lowering interest rates, government debt will be easier to pay. The conservatives reject the idea of government borrowing and say there should not be government deficits. In recent years, the liberal philosophy has held sway even among so-called conservatives. People with debts need inflation so their debts can be paid in inflated currency. A number of economic theories have been promulgated and adopted by governments and central banks around the world. This has resulted in sustained efforts to manipulate and control inflation. The Phillips Curve, Taylor Rule, Fisher Effect, and other economic theories continue to have a big impact on government actions.

The Phillips Curve

The Phillips Curve is an economic theory developed by A. W. Phillips, a New Zealander who was a professor of economics at the London School of Economics. In 1958, he came up with the idea that inflation and unemployment have a stable and inverse relationship so that when inflation goes up, unemployment declines, and vice versa. Therefore, the idea was that economic growth was accompanied by inflation and this led to more jobs and less unemployment. It was a theory that was attractive to many governments, which led them to implement a target inflation rate when economies experienced stagnant economic growth and high unemployment. The theory did not hold up in the mid-1970s when between 1973 and 1975, the US economy had six consecutive quarters of declining GDP while, at the same time, inflation numbers tripled. That was called "stagflation" and directly contradicted the Phillips Curve theory.

The Taylor Rule

First proposed in 1993 by John Taylor, a Stanford University professor, the Taylor Rule provided a guide for central banks to set nominal interest rates in response to inflation changes. The rule said that for each 1% increase in the inflation rate, the central bank would want to raise the nominal interest rate by more than 1%. Although originally not a prescription for central bank behavior – but rather a description – it soon became a rule that was followed. In any case, it was in line with conventional central banking wisdom that increasing the nominal interest rate would make the inflation rate go down, not up.

The Fisher Effect

Not all economists adhere to the idea that higher interest rates result in lower inflation and lower interest rates result in higher inflation. Basing their idea on the theories of Irving Fisher, the early twentieth-century American economist, some economists say that central banks can increase inflation by increasing, not decreasing, their nominal interest rate. Fisher, in his 1932 book *Booms and Depressions,* developed a theory which he called the "debt deflation theory of great depressions." Eventually, the idea came to be called the "Fisher effect." He described the relationship between inflation and both real and nominal interest rates. He stated that the real interest rate was equal to the nominal interest rate minus the expected inflation rate. He went on to say that recessions and depressions were due to the overall level of debt rising in real value because of deflation causing people to default on their consumer loans and mortgages. He developed the theory after the Wall Street Crash of 1929 and the Great Depression.

Inflation Targeting

The simple and politically attractive Phillips Theory was embraced around the world with the result that "inflation targeting" became an attractive action for governments. The assumption was that central banks could use interest rates to influence inflation and thereby reduce unemployment, a politically attractive action. The idea was that raising interest rates usually cooled the economy and reined in inflation, while lowering interest rates accelerated the economy, thereby boosting inflation.

Prior to the First World War, monetary policy was oriented towards adjusting exchange rates rather than inflation rates. But with the gold standard crisis after the First World War, the economist Irving Fisher suggested a currency system called a "compensated Dollar" or "commodity Dollar" where in order to sustain a constant purchasing power of the currency, the Dollar would be based on gold but the value of the gold would be determined by an index of the price of a given set of goods. This was an attempt to target price levels.

John Maynard Keynes in a 1923 paper proposed an inflation targeting scheme. With countries after the First World War experiencing inflations and deflations, he recommended a policy where currencies would be adjusted according to inflation levels.

Although Germany adopted inflation targeting earlier, in the early 1990s, the first three countries to implement fully fledged inflation targeting were New Zealand, Canada, and the United Kingdom. New Zealand pioneered inflation targeting in 1990, followed by Canada in 1991, and then the UK in 1992. In 1998, the UK's Monetary Policy Committee was given sole responsibility for setting interest rates to meet the Government's Retail Prices Index (RPI) inflation target of 2.5%. That target was changed to 2% in December 2003 when the Consumer Price Index (CPI) replaced the Retail Prices Index as the UK Treasury's inflation index.

The idea of inflation targeting spread in the 1990s to other developed countries and then to emerging economies in the 2000s.

As of 2010, it was estimated by the Bank of England's Centre for Central Banking Studies that 27 countries were "fully fledged" inflation targeters. Since that time, studies show the number has risen to 28 countries and, of course, the US and Japan also adopted the idea.

The Magic 2%

In 1998, the Governing Council of the European Central Bank (ECB) defined price stability as inflation of under 2%. Thereafter, that 2% target became standard for other major developed countries, adopted in the US in 2012 and Japan in 2013. In 2000, Frederic Mishkin – on the board of governors of the Federal Reserve System from 2006 to 2008 – and Alfred Lerner – professor of Banking and Financial Institutions at the Graduate School of Business, Columbia University – said that *although inflation targeting is not a panacea and may not be appropriate for many emerging market countries, it can be a highly useful monetary policy strategy in a number of them.* The Czech National Bank (CNB) was an example of an inflation-targeting central bank and from 2010 it used a 2% inflation target. When, in 2012, inflation was expected to fall well below the target, the CNB reduced the two-week repo rate and continued to reduce it with the intention of raising inflation. But when 0.05% was reached in late 2012, they had run out of "ammunition" and were pushing on the interest rate string. Fearing a further inflation decline and even deflation in November of 2013, the CNB said that it would weaken the Czech Koruna exchange rate against the euro. This is an example where "pushing on a string" (the interest rate string) did not work.

In 2012, US Federal Reserve chairman Ben Bernanke brought the Fed in line with other countries and set a 2% target inflation rate. Prior to that, the Federal Open Market Committee (FOMC) did not have a specific inflation target but normally announced a target range for inflation between 1.7% and 2%. When asked why they set the 2% target, Federal Reserve members said that the 2% rate was most consistent with their mandate for price stability and maximum employment, the two mandates given to them by Congress. They also said that an inflation rate that was higher than 2% would reduce the public's ability to make accurate longer-term economic and financial decisions, but a lower inflation rate would be associated with an elevated probability of falling into deflation. This would mean falling prices and wages, which were associated with weak economic conditions. They believed that having at least a small level of inflation made it less likely that the economy would fall into deflation if economic conditions weakened.

Many economists admitted that the Phillips Curve plotting the relationship between inflation and unemployment was not really well understood even if judged to be correct. But it was really a matter of faith rather than proof.

Dean Baker, an economist at the Center for Economic Policy Research, said: *"The fact that very serious economists, who enjoy great standing in the profession, could suggest a two-percentage point measurement error with a straight face shows the lack of seriousness of the discipline. People should understand what is at stake here. It is big (and simple)."*[56] Someone once said: *"Why is it 2%? Because that's the rate that over 35 years cuts in half today's dollar-purchasing power. Why would the Fed (and the government that runs it) want that to occur? It allows government to monetize the debt (i.e. pay it off with counterfeit money) without raising taxes. And inflation fools people into thinking they are progressing when their compensation rises. And it allows the government to tax the people more heavily without a direct tax increase by inflating their incomes over time."*

As well as choosing the wrong inflation measure, the inflation target set by the Fed of 2% – the amount needed to "grease the wheels" – was considered by many economists, like Baker, to be arbitrary. David Stockman, a former government economist, was one who argued that there was no scientific proof that 2% inflation was any better for growth than 1.2% or 0.02%: He said

*These are all self-serving fictions fabricated by a small
community of monetary central planners and their
Wall Street henchman, and they do one big but destructive thing. They are used to justify endless manipulation
and falsification of the single most important set of
prices in all of capitalism – the price of money and
financial assets.*[57]

Nevertheless, demands for government actions based
on the targeting theory continued. In February 2017, the
rate of inflation in the UK rose to 2.3%, above the Bank
of England's 2% target. For one leading British economist this demanded action, and a rise in interest rates: to
support savers and institution investors like pension
funds and to stop them putting their money into riskier
assets because of low bond yields.

The US Federal Reserve, with its huge stock of gold
and securities, was able to buy and sell large quantities
of securities in the open market, thus increasing or
decreasing the loanable funds in the system. When they
buy securities, they put money into circulation; and
when they sell securities, they withdraw money from
circulation. This combined with the power to raise or
lower the discount rate also meant they had a great
influence on money in the system. In 2010, Chairman
Bernanke argued that high levels of unemployment
demanded more *"quantitative easing,* a euphemism for
more cash in the system and higher inflation."* He said
that inflation needed to be around 2% *"to keep the
economy growing."*

One Federal Reserve member, John Williams, even suggested that the target be raised to 4% so that central banks could have more leeway to maneuver in an economic downturn.

At a 2018 speech before the Forecasters Club in New York, Lael Brainard, a member of the US Federal Reserve's board of governors, talked about how the federal funds rate would be adjusted to ensure that the inflation rate would be at target. She said: *"With some uptick in political uncertainty, and inflation still below target in the euro area and Japan … in the most recent data, the trailing 12-month change in core PCE prices was 1.8%, up from a year earlier, when core PCE prices increased only 1.6%. Overall PCE prices, which include the volatile food and energy sectors, increased 2.0%, largely reflecting the recent run-up in crude oil prices. While the recent core PCE data are somewhat encouraging, we will want to see inflation coming in around target on a sustained basis after seven years of below-target readings. … Re-anchoring underlying inflation at the Federal Open Market Committee's (FOMC) 2% objective is an important goal. Recent research has highlighted the downside risks to inflation and inflation expectations that are posed by the effective lower bound on nominal interest rates, and it underscores the importance of ensuring underlying inflation does not slip below target in today's new normal."*[58]

Speech, Chairman Ben S. Bernanke *Monetary Policy Objectives and Tools in a Low-Inflation Environment*, October 15, 2010.

In 2018, Fed Chairman Jerome H. Powell's appearance before the House Financial Services Committee
was his first as the powerful chairman of the world's
most influential central bank. Commentators said that
the Fed had been aiming to boost inflation to 2%, but
the recent pickup in monthly readings had spooked
some investors who worried the central bank might
overshoot its target. He said: *"Despite the recent volatility, financial conditions remain accommodative. At the
same time, inflation remains below our 2% longer-run
objective. In the FOMC's view, further gradual increases
in the federal funds rate will best promote attainment of
both of our objectives."*[59] In his testimony, Powell
described the risks to the economic outlook as "roughly
balanced," but noted that officials would monitor
inflation closely.

The Low Inflation Trap

According to some economists, a severe problem arises
when inflation reaches zero. This is the so-called "low
inflation trap." Many macroeconomists believed that
short-term interest rates could not go below zero because
if interest rates were negative, people would prefer to
hold cash. Central bankers would then respond to this by
reducing the nominal interest rate. But the so-called
Fisher Effect would result in lower inflation, causing
further reductions in the nominal interest rate by the

central bank. Finally, when the central bank sets the nominal interest rate at zero, nothing else can be done and they are stuck in a low-inflation trap from which they can't escape, according to the theory. Unfortunately, it is not only a theory since we have seen this happen in reality in Japan. The Bank of Japan, from 1995, experienced an average inflation rate of about zero despite its inflation target of 2%. But it was a trap and they were unable to get out of despite extraordinary and unprecedented increased money supply measures which probably did more harm than good.

Even the Europeans encountered the low inflation policy trap condition in 2018. During that year, the European Central Bank had a nominal interest rate at 0.34% and a negative inflation rate at –0.23%, the Swedish Riksbank had a key nominal interest rate of below zero at –0.50% and an inflation rate of 0.79%; the Danish Central Bank had a negative interest rate of –0.23% and inflation rate of 0%; the Swiss National Bank had a negative nominal interest rate of –0.73% and inflation rate of –0.35%; and the Bank of England had a nominal interest rate of 0.47% and inflation rate of 0.30%. Each of these central banks had been missing their inflation target in some instances for a long period of time. Even the US Fed could be included since the Fed fund's rate was targeted at close to zero for about seven years, up to December of 2015 when it was increased to between 0.25 and 0.50%.

So, you might say that these bankers were trapped and were being forced to abandon the Taylor Rule and instead adopt the ideas of the Neo-Fisherites. But the actions they had taken included pushing market nominal interest rates below zero and charging a fee on reserves kept at the central bank (essentially a negative interest). This was done by the Bank of Japan, the Swiss National Bank, the Danish Central Bank, and the Swedish Riksbank. Another action would be "quantitative easing" (QE) where the central bank purchased long-maturity assets such as government debt and private assets as mortgage-backed securities and even equities, as the Bank of Japan had done through its purchases of Exchange Traded Funds (ETFs) of Japanese shares. Another action central banks can take is to engage in a kind of psychological warfare where they give "forward guidance" that they hope ensures that interest rates stay low in the future. They can do this in the hope that it will increase inflation. In Switzerland, negative interest rates resulted in lower inflation and eventually deflation. The QE action did not work either. This was seen in Japan where an aggressive program of buying assets did not result in higher inflation.

Argentina: Lies, Damned Lies

In 2006, Argentinian President Nestor Kirchner summoned the executives from major companies such as

Procter & Gamble, Unilever, and Kimberly-Clark and ordered them to stop raising prices. He negotiated agreements that required companies to freeze prices for as long as a year to help the government fight inflation. In 2005, Kirchner called for a national boycott of Royal Dutch Shell after it raised prices to offset the surge in international oil costs. Of course, under such circumstances, companies were also trying to survive by introducing new products or old products in a new form which carried a higher price point.

As mentioned earlier, in 2006, the repercussions of Kirchner's efforts to control inflation had a life-changing impact on Graciela Bevacqua, director of INDEC – the Instituto Nacional de Exadistica y Censos – Argentina's national statistics agency. She recalled: *"As soon as Moreno was appointed he summoned me and my immediate supervisor to his office. When we entered the room, I became scared. He had put on classical music, and I thought it was because he didn't want people outside to hear what he was doing."*

Bevacqua had been working there since 1984, beginning as an independent contractor and working her way up to director in 2002. Throughout her time there, she had been part of the team responsible for the country's Consumer Price Index (CPI), which was used to measure the country's rate of inflation.

Over those two decades, the Argentinian economy had enjoyed, if that is the word, something of a rollercoaster

ride. In the late 1970s and early 1980s, the economy had
suffered under the then military dictatorship, with over
400,000 companies going bankrupt and financial liberali-
zation increasing the debt burden substantially. The subsequent neoliberal economic policies, which dominated
until the end of the 1990s, did little to dent this.

The country suffered from 15 years of stagflation –
that painful combination of stagnant growth and inflation that at the end of the 1980s led to a period of
hyperinflation. In May 1989, inflation reached 96% and
riots broke out as basic foodstuffs rocketed in price. In
the 1990s, the government managed to get this under
control (inflation returning to single figures) via a mix-
ture of deregulation, privatization, and limiting the
growth of the money supply. But then the economic
crisis hit again: between 1998 and 2002, Argentina's
GDP declined by 20%, its currency depreciated by
70%, and it defaulted on the debt on which it was
reliant. The early 1990s, by contrast, saw Argentina
using expansionary policies to reboot the country –
creating five million jobs and boosting investment. In
the decade after the economic crisis, the Argentinian
economy almost doubled, growing at 9% between 2003
and 2007. After years of being a country of economic
instability, Argentina finally seemed to have turned a
corner, and become an attractive proposition for investors around the world.

But was this economic success story everything that it seemed? The flipside of the expansionary policies that the Argentinian economy was pursuing was the risk of the return of inflation. And here, Graciela Bevacqua, dutifully doing her calculations of the CPI, was beginning to find her work questioned by the government. *"In hindsight,"* she told the Royal Statistical Society in 2012, *"it is now apparent that problems began as early as 2005 when a newly appointed Minister of Economics began questioning the CPI figures which we were providing. For 2005 the CPI was estimated to be 12.3% and on an upward trend."*[60]

This was not news the government wanted to hear – or, indeed, wanted foreign investors to hear. The following year, with the appointment of Guillermo Moreno as Secretary of Domestic Trade, the situation got worse: *"He began a tirade,"* Bevacqua recalls of their first meeting, *"about how the consumer price index affected people's morale and the effectiveness can successfully implement policies that increase confidence in the economic outlook … he said that if we didn't aim for zero inflation, we were unpatriotic. He told us that the patriotic thing to do was to report a low CPI (or at least a CPI on a downward trend) and that it was the duty of INDEC to cooperate with the government to make sure that the CPI would be favorable."*[60]

It was an extraordinary demand and one at odds with both Bevacqua's integrity and also what the CPI statistics were about: they were there to reflect accurately the state of the economy, not to be manipulated for political ends. Over the following years, the demands on Bevacqua continued. The government wanted a list of the companies that INDEC used to create their inflation's figures so they could be leaned on, too. They asked for changes made to how the figures were calculated: in terms of bread prices, they wanted a greater weighting for supermarket bread, despite the fact that the vast majority of bread was bought from local bakers; for holiday prices, they wanted various destinations removed from the list. Moreno even demanded that the figures be rounded down: so, both 2.599 and 2.501 would both be rounded down to 2.5. It was a small change that made a significant difference when compounded.

Bevacqua held firm, so Moreno fired her in January 2007. When the inflation figures came out for January the following month, the announced rate showed a significant drop. Over the following years, the newly worked government figures showed a marked deceleration in rising prices: for 2007, inflation was more manageable at 8.5%. The government's success story of economic growth and controllable inflation – the opposite of the stagflation years of the 1980s – continued.

Bevacqua, however, was far from finished. Calling in a group of Buenos Aires economics students, she started to compile her own inflation data. Her numbers were significantly different from the official ones: rather than inflation being 8.5% in 2007, Bevacqua estimated that the real inflation figure was three times that number, at 25%. The implications of this were substantial, to say the least. A report for the *Washington Post* in 2009 suggested that the underreported figures were *"… cheating investors of proper compensation on nearly $50 billion in debt benchmarked to inflation."* The article quoted Robert Shapiro, co-chair of the American Task Force Argentina, who explained that *"the way these bonds work is that every month, or every six months, the principal adjusts for inflation. So, if inflation is actually 30%, and they're only adjusting 10%, that's a huge loss."*[61]

The government tried to shut down Bevacqua and various other consultancies who were also compiling their own inflation figures. In March 2011, they were each fined $125,000 for compiling statistics that didn't comply with "appropriate methodological requirements" – a somewhat ironic charge for a government that was, as *The Economist* described in a 2011 article, "Cooking the Books." But Moreno went further still: Bevacqua was charged with publishing figures based on false information, with the aim of distorting the market. If found guilty, she faced a prison sentence of two to six years: the judge, to the government's frustration, dismissed the case.

Despite the Argentinian government's efforts, their figures were becoming increasingly discredited.

The Economist stopped including Argentina's figures in their monthly summaries, saying: *"since 2007 Argentina has published inflation figures that almost nobody believes … we have decided to drop INDEC's figures entirely. We are tired of being an unwilling party to what appears to be a deliberate attempt to deceive voters and swindle investors."*[60]

Previously, the Argentinian government had tried dramatic efforts to control inflation. In 1985, with runaway inflation, it changed its currency, replacing the Peso with the Austral. Initially, the Austral was worth more than the USD, but by the beginning of 1989, it had reached levels of 11 or 12 to the USD. By 1989, Argentina was experiencing massive inflation of 5,000% and an austerity plan including a currency devaluation of the Austral by 11% against the USD and an agreement with businesses to keep prices frozen for two weeks and then limited increases after that. In order to cope with inflation that was running at 25% per month, government employees would get a salary increase of about that much. Also, there was a 30% increase in public utility rates and transit fares as well as cutbacks in government spending. But the plan was apparently not very credible since almost immediately, merchants began raising prices. In May of 1989, the government imposed price freezes in order to right the inflation, but the measures were hardly credible and prices continued to rise on the black market. Despite fixing a special Austral exchange rate for exports at 36 Australs per USD, in two months the rate rose to as high as 105 to the USD. Car prices doubled in one month and such items as disposable diapers went from 250 Australs a pack to 1,200 per pack in three weeks. Meanwhile, the Argentine Mint printing presses were working overtime to print nine million 1,000 denomination Austral bills, the highest denomination. Restrictions were imposed on withdrawals from banks. In April 1990, 80,000 civil servants were forced to retire. By that time, the annual inflation had risen to 20,000%.

In other meetings with government officials, agreements had been negotiated for them to freeze prices for one year as an aid to the government's fight against inflation. But even then, economists were predicting that the effort would be a waste of higher government spending and central bank purchases of Dollars aimed at weakening the local currency.

Brazil Anti-Inflation Efforts

In February of 1986, Brazil's President Jose Sarney, in an effort to stop inflation, introduced a new currency, the Cruzado, to replace the old currency, the Cruzeiro, which had lasted for almost 20 years but had experienced a massive fall against the US Dollar. The new currency,

Cruzado, cut off three zeros in its exchange against the Cruzeiro. At first, the plan seemed to work, but when the government failed to control its own spending, inflation eventually skyrocketed as sellers began to sell their goods on the black market instead of at the official prices which did not cover their costs. In January of 1989, with inflation running at 1,000%, Sarney introduced another anti-inflation package nicknamed the "Summer Plan" for the season in which it was introduced. The plan included another Brazilian currency, the New Cruzado, replacing the previous Cruzado, making the old currency worth one-thousandth of its face value. He also imposed wage and price freezes as well as layoffs of 60,000 government employees. Almost immediately, the new currency started to fall against the USD. Merchants all over Brazil started raising prices in order to beat the planned price freeze. At the same time, the government announced price increases on electricity, postage, and telephone service which at that time were controlled by government enterprises. Higher prices were set for such items as bread, milk, gasoline, and other basics. Wages were being adjusted in a formula to take into account the average inflation over the previous 12 months, but then would be frozen. The new measure was followed by strikes with a reported 800,000 federal workers walking out of their jobs in protest at low wages.

In April of 1990, President Fernando Collor de Mello received Brazil's Congress approval to implement a controversial anti-inflation plan which at the time was considered one of the most draconian monetary reforms in history to confront the 4,800% inflation the country was experiencing. Strict limits were placed on how much money Brazilians could withdraw from bank and savings accounts over the following 18 months to drastically reduce the money supply. It was estimated that the measure froze about US$115 billion of the US$150 billion in individual and company accounts. Of course, the freezing of bank accounts created all kinds of problems, such as making it difficult for companies to pay wages.

In February of 1991, Brazilians were faced with the government's action to freeze wages and prices indefinitely for the fifth time in five years in an attempt to kill inflation. At the same time, their despair increased. Economy Minister Zélia Cardoso de Mello also announced rises of up to 71% on fuel, electricity, telephone, and postal charges. With inflation running at 20% a month, it was a last-ditch attempt to stop inflation; but the government was faced with a lack of credibility. Under the Cruzado Plan in 1986, initially people believed that it might work and went to shops to check prices and prevent any increases; but by the time of the fourth price freeze, very few believed that it would work. Adding to the disbelief was that, as part of its drive to cut the federal payroll, the Collor government had dismantled the departments which formerly monitored and checked prices! Critics also pointed out the contradiction between Collor's expressed aim of making Brazil a totally free market economy and his government's increasing interventionism.

Chinese Government Efforts to Control Inflation

In May 2011, the Chinese authorities criticized Unilever PLC for talking publicly about planned price increases which resulted in a scramble for products like soap and detergent. The National Development and Reform Commission, China's economic planning agency, fined Unilever about $300,000 saying that the company had broken the law when it spread information about impending price increases and disrupted the "market order." At the time, the government was battling mounting inflation which had hit 5.4% in March 2011. Unilever and other companies had been asked by the government to refrain from price increases.

In April 2011, the People's Bank of China, the country's central bank, increased the reserve requirements of banks in order to reduce the amount of money available for lending. They hoped that by taking such measures, they could halt the rising inflation rate. One economist said that hiking the reserve requirement was the most effective and direct way to fight against inflation caused by "hot money." Another researcher said that the government should take tighter and more effective measures, including higher interest rate rises.

In 2012, Jim Chanos, the head of Kynikos Associates and the man famous for predicting the Enron collapse, claimed that a similar situation was also unfolding in China. In an interview with CNN, he claimed, *"One of the things I'm pretty convinced of based on our analysis is that inflation is under-reported in China by as much as 4 to 5% a year."* As with Argentina, if the inflation figures were wrong, then this would also apply to the levels of economic growth the country was enjoying (at the time, in the 9–10% range).

Chanos suspected that the official government statistics were masking the real situation: *"We are seeing rapid falloffs in demand in things like construction equipment, railway construction over there, housing sales – so lots of things are slowing down pretty quickly over there. It remains to be seen whether that's going to go into a full-fledged recession. I do think the property sector, which is where we're focused on, is going to enter – or has entered a recession."*[62]

Once again, there were clearly strong implications for anyone investing in the country. But there were implications, too, for domestic economic policy. In Argentina, the lower inflation rates meant that anyone negotiating an inflation-linked wage demand was not going to get an increase that actually reflected the real economic situation. In China, a lower inflation rate meant that China's central bank could look at loosening monetary policy by lowering its interest rates: this would have advantages in terms of stimulating the economy, but higher inflation rates (and higher interest rates) would make that more difficult.

Philippines Data Control

In addition to all the pitfalls of obtaining data from individuals who may give the wrong facts, or who maybe shy from revealing items about their spending, there's also the problem of extracting data from the government departments who collect it. I had one experience in the Philippines where the Philippine government Department of Trade and Industry through their website denied my request for data from 2004 and 2014 of a number of items other than food products. The Philippine Statistics Authority also was resistant and did not provide the information I requested. Even the Philippines' Freedom of Information website said that besides the agricultural food products information that they provided, other information was only for their internal use. When I asked for information regarding prices of bicycles, automobiles, TVs, etc. and the Department of Trade and Industry refused to provide that data.

Venezuela – Eliminating a Bill

In December 2016, it was reported that President Nicolás Maduro appeared to have created a huge demand for the country's slumping national currency, the Bolivar, in a country with the world's highest inflation rate as a result of mass printing of Bolivares. But then the President went on television and announced that the country's largest denomination 100 banknote, estimated to represent 80% of the cash in the country, would cease to be legal tender within 72 hours. This resulted in a wild scramble for smaller bills and a strengthening of the exchange rate against the USD. But people were not cheering because, with no shops accepting 100 bills, people were short of cash to buy anything for the coming holidays; and in some Venezuelan cities, riots broke out and stores were looted. Using the common ploy of country leaders faced with a crisis, Maduro blamed the "international mafias" waging a US-directed "economic war" against the country by hoarding 100-Bolivar notes and taking them over the border into Colombia. One economist said: *"Tightening monetary policy by taking out four-fifths of an economy's cash is like killing a mosquito with a flamethrower."* The move by Maduro did not change the underlying problems driving inflation including a decline in productivity, falling oil revenue, and soaring debt.

In March of 2017, Venezuela halted publication of money supply data, a tool to ascertain the level of the soaring inflation. The previous year, it had stopped issuing inflation data in order to hide the triple-digit inflation. The M2 money supply indicator was up almost 180% in February from a year earlier before the release of the data was halted: M2 was the sum of cash together with checking, savings, and other deposits. The skyrocketing of M2, combined with a decline in the output of goods and services, was fueling the hyperinflation.

India Control Efforts

In 2008, India's inflation was rising and the government faced a deteriorating fiscal position. The Reserve Bank of India (RBI, the central bank) raised the benchmark lending rate to the highest in more than five years, making the move in the belief that it would halt the rising inflation. Officials of the bank said that they would act "decisively, effectively, and swiftly" to curb inflation.

In May of 2008, the Indian government was challenged with higher inflation numbers. The inflation rate had been hovering above 7%, well above the government's comfort zone. One response was to subsidize fuel prices. Another part of the policy was to strengthen the Rupee by buying Rupees with $300 billion of foreign reserves (it was estimated that for a 1% rise in the value of the Rupee, the Wholesale Price Index would fall by 0.2% accordingly). Furthermore, they considered that futures markets were contributing to the rise in food prices and, therefore, banned futures trading in rice, wheat, soy oil, chickpeas, potatoes, and rubber. Critics of the move said that it would make things worse since valuable market-pricing mechanisms would be lost and traders would move to the untaxed and unregulated black market. They said that the suspension was a politically motivated act in view of the upcoming national election and the ruling coalition was responding to left-wing partners who were clamoring for action to reduce prices of essential commodities. They added that it was a surprise since the government-appointed committee had found that there was no conclusive evidence that futures trading drove up prices. At that time, the average daily volume traded on the National Commodities and Derivatives Exchange, the main market for agricultural futures, was $600 million compared to India's overall agricultural output of $129,000 million in 2006. Given the small size of the futures market, they said that it had little effect and also could easily be manipulated with relatively small amounts of money. Despite the domestic ban on futures trading, there were rumors that the government had quietly placed an order on wheat futures on the Chicago Board of Trade in order to have options in case of domestic shortages.

Korea: Consumer Pressure

In 2012, consumers in Korea protested against price hikes by McDonald's and other foreign multinationals who were not obeying government efforts to restrict rising consumer prices. Although the price changes were a few percent, consumers noticed them and responded. Students, in particular, were sensitive to fast food prices since they were regular customers. In 2011, candy manufacturers such as the giants Orion and Lotte Confectionery faced harsh criticism when they raised prices. The politicians were active as well and, in 2008, President Lee Myung-bak ordered that 52 daily essentials, including general commodities and consumer goods, be put under close watch. But observers noticed that even after the price hikes, demand had not diminished.

Bottom Line

The multiple, and sometimes opposing, theories as to what drives inflation are another indication that, even today, we still lack a complete understanding of this phenomenon. What is clear, however, is that inflation is immensely important to politicians. High inflation can break their necks, as voters are left frustrated with their purchasing power diminishing continuously. So, while governments in the best case try to control inflation (and in the worst case manipulate the numbers) to keep their voters happy, they base their decisions on incomplete information with sometimes disastrous consequences. At the same time, politicians cling to the belief that a 2% inflation target is beneficial to the economy, while anything else poses a danger. However, there is no proof that this is actually the case. On the one hand, politicians fear too high inflation; on the other, some are wary of deflation, which they see as a sign of a contraction in economic activity. When it comes to the threat of deflation, as you will see in the next chapter, I do not quite agree.

8 The Wonderful World of Deflation

Deflation is the opposite of inflation with falling instead of rising prices. It's a much-feared phenomenon by many economists who think that declining prices will ruin economic growth, make it more difficult to pay back debts, and result in consumers delaying spending in the expectation that prices will continue to fall. As I have mentioned, in order to avoid deflation, central bankers have attempted to increase the money supply by purchasing bonds and other assets from the market and issuing cash in exchange in order to supply the market with liquidity. At the same time, they have lowered interest rates, even allowed those rates to move into negative territory, so people and businesses will be encouraged to borrow and spend, leading to a rise in prices and avoidance of deflation.

What the Experts Say:

Like the topic of inflation, many famous authors and
economists have had something to say about deflation.
Those opinions have fallen into the following general
categories.

Monetary Policy Can't Control Inflation

*Toshihiko Fukui, former governor of the Bank of Japan:
*"However, in spite of the general perception that monetary
policy should be conducted so as to avert deflation, a central
bank cannot lower interest rates below the zero lower
bound."*[63]

Deflation Should Be Prevented

*Ben Bernanke, former chairman of the US Federal
Reserve: *"The basic prescription for preventing deflation is
straightforward, at least in principle: Use monetary and
fiscal policy as needed to support aggregate spending, in a
manner as nearly consistent as possible with full utilization
of economic resources and low and stable inflation. In other
words, the best way to get out of trouble is not to get into it
in the first place."*[35]

Deflation Benefits Debtholders and Property Owners

*Michael Hudson, Wall Street financial analyst: *"When
there's deflation, it means that although most markets are*

shrinking, and people have less to spend, the 1% that hold the 99% in debt are getting all the growth in wealth and income. Deflation means that income is being transferred to the 1%, that is, to the creditors and property owners."[64]

Technology Is Causing Deflation

*Ken Moelis, founder of Moelis & Company: *"A big secular thing going on is technology and deflation. This is where I think millennials are getting that it is an improvement in life, and they're taking advantage of it.*"[65]

*Jim Grant, founder of Grant's Interest Rate Observer: *"Thanks to the spread of electricity and other such wonders in the final quarter of the 19th century, prices dwindled year by year at a rate of 1.5% to 2% per year. People didn't call it deflation – they called it progress.*"[66]

Deflation Is Bad for People in Debt

*Michael Hudson, Wall Street financial analyst: *"There are two definitions of deflation. Most people think of it simply as prices going down. But debt deflation is what happens when people have to spend more and more of their income to carry the debts that they've run up – to pay their mortgage debt, to pay the credit card debt, to pay student loans.*"[64]

*Ben Bernanke, former chairman of the US Federal Reserve: *"Deflation can be particularly dangerous when a financial system is shaky, with household and corporate balance sheets in poor shape and banks undercapitalized and heavily burdened with bad loans."*[34]

Deflation is a Decrease in Money Supply and Credit

*Mish Shedlock, investment advisor representative for Sitka Pacific Capital Management: *"Deflation properly defined is a net decrease in the money supply and credit, with credit being marked to market. Deflation by that measure went global long ago."*[67]

*Murray N. Rothbard, economist, historian, and political theorist: *"'Deflation' is usually defined as generally falling prices, yet it can also be defined as a decline in the money supply which, of course, will also tend to lower prices. It is particularly important to distinguish between changes in prices or the money supply that arise from voluntary changes in people's values or actions on the free market; as against deliberate changes in the money supply imposed by governmental coercion."*[68]

Central Banks Cause Deflation

*Peter Cresswell: *"There are two kinds of 'deflation': progressive and destructive. Central banks and their 'stabilisation' make the first impossible, and the second more likely."*[69]

Deflation Is Caused by an Increased Production of Goods and Services

*George Reisman, professor emeritus of economics at Pepperdine University: *"Deflation is usually thought to be a synonym for falling prices. There could be no more serious error in all of economics. Calling falling prices 'deflation' results in a profound confusion between prosperity and depression. This is because the leading cause of falling prices is economic progress, whose essential feature is an increasing production and supply of goods and services, which, of course, operates to make prices fall."*[70]

People Should Accept Deflation

*Carlos Ghosn, chairman and CEO of Groupe Renault: *"To face deflation, you have to have people accepting it and not reacting to it."*[71]

Deflation Is Bad

*Robert Kiyosaki, founder of Rich Dad Company: *"Deflation isn't good, and inflation is easier to cure than deflation."*[29]

*Lawrence Summers, former director of the National Economic Council: *"Deflation and secular stagnation are the macroeconomic threat of our time."*[72]

*Jack Kemp, former US secretary of housing and urban development: *"The real problem is deflation. That is the opposite of inflation but equally serious to the borrower."*[73]

*Gavyn Davies, chairman of Fulcrum Asset Management: *"Inflation is now always the main problem, or indeed a problem at all. Sometimes, though rarely, deflation is a more serious threat, and we need to shelve many of the orthodoxies we have held so dear."*[74]

*Ben Bernanke, former chairman of the US Federal Reserve: *"The sources of deflation are not a mystery. Deflation is in almost all cases a side effect of a collapse of aggregate demand – a drop in spending so severe that producers must cut prices on an ongoing basis in order to find buyers. Likewise, the economic effects of a deflationary episode, for the most part, are similar to those of any other sharp decline in aggregate spending – namely, recession, rising unemployment, and financial stress."*[35]

Deflation is Good

*Mish Shedlock, investment advisor representative for Sitka Pacific Capital Management: *"You should not be afraid of deflation. You should be afraid of policies attempting to fight it."*[75]

The Trend towards Lower Prices and Rising Incomes

In recent years, the impact of large retail firms such as Wal Mart, Target in the US, Aldi in Europe, and others – in addition to online platforms like Amazon and Alibaba – have resulted in lower or at least stable prices for a wide range of goods, despite the inflationary policies being implemented by central banks. Pricing power has shifted away from the manufacturer to the distribution retailers, offline and online. There has also been a revolution in product improvements so that former luxury items such as cars, mobile phones, computers, and the internet are now common goods and services enjoyed by millions.

The UN Food and Agriculture Office tracks prices of food around the world, converts local prices to US Dollars, and calculates an index with 100 being the average for 2002–04. Prices for meats, cereals, oils/fats, dairy, and sugar make up the components of the monthly updated index. Of course, commonly, the currencies used to quote these prices are being depreciated by their governments, including in the US where the supply of Dollars is being increased as more credit and currency is released. As the currency depreciation accelerates, there is an apparent increase in the cost of food. But technology and capital are being applied daily to reduce the cost of growing and shipping food everywhere in the world. As fertilizers and pest controllers are improved, as machinery makes agriculture more efficient, and as distribution processes are enhanced with cold chains and faster transport, food is more readily available and of better quality. These changes result in falling prices, or at least stabilized prices despite currency depreciation.

The transformation of food distribution in Turkey is an example of how prices have not kept pace with higher incomes. For many years, high food inflation was perceived to be a chronic problem. Then the government took steps to overhaul the wholesale food trading and retailing system to increase competition and reduce intermediary costs. One impact of these measures was the weight of "food and beverages" in the CPI dropped to 23% in 2018 from 31% in 1994. It was naturally found that food costs rose when there was waste because of the lack of cold storage and poor packing. This problem was gradually being solved as a result of organized modern retailing. However, a lot still needed to be done, since although 40% of food retailing was in the organized modern retail system, the remaining 60% was still sold in open bazaars where cold storage was not available. Also, there was a need to reduce the number of middlemen between the farmer and the consumer. Changes were underway. The rise of online shopping, for example, was having an impact on eliminating the many distribution steps, thus resulting in lower prices and enhanced quality.

Food and Gold

Charles Vollum studied the money systems of many countries and began to realize the importance of having a standard of value not tied to any country's currency and monetary policy. He theorized that, in fact, rising and falling "gold prices" were really more accurately viewed as falling and rising "currency prices," measured against the relative stability of gold. This insight led to the founding of Gold Monocle Group, Ltd, and the creation of the Priced in Gold website in 2007. He studied the price of food in gold terms in order to control for the different and varied currency movements. With the constant devaluation of currency, he concluded that gold was a common long-term value instrument. He found that if food was measured in terms of ounces of gold, then there was evidence of massive deflation. In 2002, the FAO (Food and Agriculture Organization) Food Price Index was 120 in gold terms but, by 2017, it was about 50. During that time, the gold price went from about $280 per ounce in 2002 to $1,290 in 2017 (Figure 8.1).

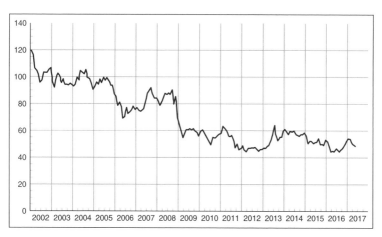

Figure 8.1 FAO Food Price Index in Gold (2002–04=100) Monthly from January 2002 to June 2017

Productivity and Deflation

Those who worry about deflation often fail to recognize the impact of productivity. At the time when there was concern in the United States over the Federal Reserve raising interest rates in the face of higher inflation indicated by higher wages and lower unemployment, productivity improvements were overlooked. Even under conditions of full employment, companies could realize more output from each worker. This growth in output per worker or increase in productivity in recent years has not been exceptional – or at least that's what the numbers seem to indicate. But a close look shows that productivity is rising not only in manufacturing but also in the service industries. With investments in robotics and labor-saving machines, generally, productivity is bound to rise. In the service industry, we only have to look at the retail trade with such technologies as voice and facial recognition as well as digital wireless payments to see how these technologies have improved productivity and service quality.

Productivity is a key feature of rising incomes and economic growth generally. The most amazing development in recent years has been the accelerated diffusion of knowledge around the world as a result of better communications, evidenced by the spread of the internet and particularly by the lower cost and wider distribution of smartphones. More importantly, while in the past the key knowledge driving productivity came primarily from the United States, Europe, and Japan – the so-called developed countries – now more and more innovation is coming from emerging countries such as China, India, Brazil, Russia, and others.

In late 2015, looking at the R&D expenditures in various countries, it could be seen that China was already approaching the $500 billion that the US was spending on R&D each year. Chinese expenditures were expected to exceed that amount in the not-too-distant future. In addition, the number of patents registered by emerging market countries was moving up at a very rapid pace. Of course, it's natural to expect this phenomenon to occur as knowledge reaches the most populated parts of the world, such as India and China – each with over 1 billion people. We can expect that these countries will expand on the knowledge acquired from the United States, European countries, and Japan. They will then move one rung higher up the knowledge and innovation ladder.

Technology and Deflation

Advances in technology have seen prices fall dramatically in some sectors. When DVD players were launched commercially in 1997, they cost USD $1,000. By 2000, the price had fallen to $100; three years later, they were available for $50; by 2018, a new player could cost as little as $20. This is not a new phenomenon: the Great Deflation of the 1870s and 1880s was also driven by reduced prices resulting from technological advancements, leading to growth in countries like the US, and difficulties for more established industrial nations like the UK who were confronted with competition from the growth productivity of the US.

Computer power costs have also dropped dramatically: $1,000 of computer equipment in 1900 bought a fraction of the calculations per second that are achieved now. Storage prices in terms of cost per gigabyte in the late 1950s were about $1,000,000, while by 2017 they had dropped to less than $0.1. At the same time, hard drive storage capacity went from about 0.01 gigabytes (GB) to well over 1,000 GB.

The impact of technology on the cost of things is easy enough to determine in a number of ways. For example, if we compare online and offline consumer goods sales, we can see a significant difference (Figure 8.2). Kleiner Perkins has done a study comparing consumer product prices for matching products online and offline between the 1st quarter of 2016 and the 1st quarter of 2018, while offline prices came down by about 1%. The online prices fell by 3%.

In the hospitality business, we can see that there has been a large increase in the use of shared space. Airbnb

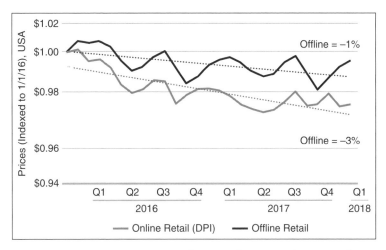

Figure 8.2 Consumer Prices for Matching Products: Online vs. Offline Source: Data from Kleiner Perkins: https://www. kleinerperkins.com/.76

guest arrivals and active listings by hosts between 2009 and 2018 grew dramatically. Guest arrivals went from almost nothing in 2009 to 80,000,000, while in the same period active listings went from practically nothing to about 5,000,000 (Figure 8.3).

The impact on overnight accommodations was quite remarkable with Airbnb offering substantially lower rates for overnight accommodations. For example, in New York City, the average room price in hotels as of January 2018 was about $306 while the Airbnb average was $187. In Sydney, the average hotel rate was $240 while the Airbnb rate was $191. In Tokyo, the difference was extraordinary, with hotel rates averaging $220 while

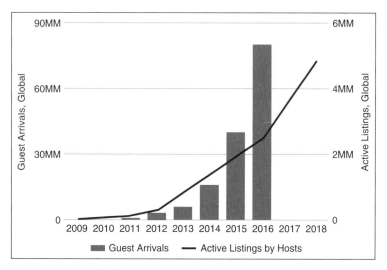

Figure 8.3 Airbnb Guest Arrivals & Active Listings by Hosts 5MM Global Active Listings Source: Data from Airbnb: https://www.airbnb.com/.[77]

the Airbnb rate was $93. Differences could be seen in other cities such as London, Toronto, Paris, Moscow, and Berlin (Figure 8.4).

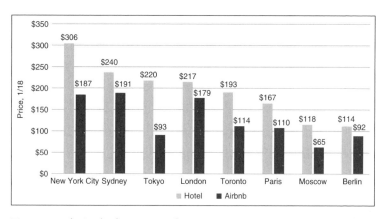

Figure 8.4 Airbnb vs. Hotel: Average Room Price per Night Source: Data from Airbnb: https://www.airbnb.com/.[77]

When it comes to transportation, the advent of Uber and other online transport services are driving down the cost of transportation. During 2017, in New York City, the average weekly commute costs were $218, while the UberX and Uber Pool cost was $142; in Chicago, the difference was $116 versus $77; in Washington DC, it was $130 versus $96. In Los Angeles, the average personal car cost was $89, while the UberX and Uber Pool average cost were $62. It was only in Dallas, Texas where the difference was reversed. The personal car weekly commute costs in that city came to an average of $65, while the UberX and Uber Pool costs were $181. Of course, that was cheaper than New York for Uber, but Dallas seems to be a substantial outlier and not typical of what was found elsewhere (Figure 8.5).

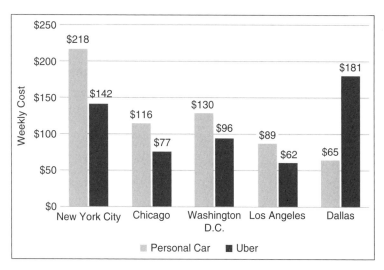

Figure 8.5 UberX/POOL vs. Personal Car: Weekly Commute Costs in the Five Largest USA Cities, 2017 Source: Data from Uber: https://www.uber.com/[78]

Deflation is Next Door – Singapore and Malaysia Prices

In 2018, people living in Singapore could take a quick one-hour trip across the border to Johor in Malaysia and find that prices for the same items were half or less than in Singapore. The price differences were quite remarkable. So, someone with a car or a bus ticket could travel to Johor from Singapore within the hour or two the trip required, and immediately reduce their inflation by half or more. (Table 8.1: RM=Malaysian Ringgit, S$=Singapore Dollar.)

Deflating the World's Fair

I often come across articles comparing what something cost in the past and what it would cost today using government inflation numbers. One study reported on the internet site Yahoo, *What it Would Cost Today,* focused on the 1939 World's Fair at Flushing Meadows New York. This is particularly close to my heart because I was a 2-year-old being carried around that 1939 World's Fair and vaguely remember the big buildings and crowds. As a working man with a modest salary, my father must have considered it quite a luxury to bring his whole family: my mother, me, and two older brothers. Using an online inflation calculator provided by the Federal Reserve Bank of Minneapolis, the article

Table 8.1 Malaysia and Singapore Price Difference, May 2018

	Malaysia	Singapore	Difference
Meal, inexpensive restaurant, 2 people	10.00 RM (3.38 S$)	44.41 RM (15.00 S$)	+344%
McMeal at McDonald's	13.00 RM (4.39 S$)	23.39 RM (7.90 S$)	+80%
Domestic beer (0.5 liter draught)	13.50 RM (4.56 S$)	29.60 RM (10.00 S$)	+119%
Coke/Pepsi (0.33 liter bottle)	2.27 RM (0.77 S$)	5.11 RM (1.73 S$)	+125%
Water (0.33 liter bottle)	1.28 RM (0.43 S$)	3.86 RM (1.30 S$)	+201%
Milk (regular, 1 liter)	6.86 RM (2.32 S$)	9.26 RM (3.13 S$)	+35%
Rice (white, 1 kg)	3.94 RM (1.33 S$)	8.38 RM (2.83 S$)	+113%
Eggs (regular, 12)	5.22 RM (1.76 S$)	8.29 RM (2.80 S$)	+59%
Apples (1 kg)	9.97 RM (3.37 S$)	13.64 RM (4.61 S$)	+37%
Bananas (1 kg)	5.30 RM (1.79 S$)	8.20 RM (2.77 S$)	+55%
Tomatoes (1 kg)	4.71 RM (1.59 S$)	8.06 RM (2.72 S$)	+71%
Taxi start (normal tariff)	3.00 RM (1.01 S$)	10.36 RM (3.50 S$)	+245%
Gasoline (1 liter)	2.22 RM (0.75 S$)	6.59 RM (2.23 S$)	+197%
Volkswagen Golf 1.4 90 KW (or equivalent new car)	148,466.25 RM (50,149.06 S$)	355,259.90 RM (120,000.00 S$)	+139%
Basic (electricity, heating, cooling, water, garbage) for 85 m^2 apartment	181.53 RM (61.32 S$)	431.64 RM (145.80 S$)	+138%

(Continued)

Table 8.1 (Continued)

	Malaysia	Singapore	Difference
1 min. of prepaid mobile tariff local (no discounts or plans)	0.26 RM (0.09 S$)	0.47 RM (0.16 S$)	+84%
Internet (60 Mbps or more, unlimited data, cable/DSL)	163.24 RM (55.14 S$)	138.32 RM (46.72 S$)	-15%
Fitness club, monthly free for 1 adult	140.58 RM (47.49 S$)	407.48 RM (137.64 S$)	+190%
Cinema, international release, 1 seat	15.00 RM (5.07 S$)	35.53 RM (12.00 S$)	+137%
Preschool (or kindergarten), full day, private, monthly for 1 child	619.38 RM (209.21 S$)	2,828.03 RM (955.26 S$)	+357%
1 pair of jeans (Levi's 501 or similar)	218.93 RM (73.95 S$)	286.73 RM (96.85 S$)	+31%
1 pair of men's leather business shoes	258.82 RM (87.42 S$)	394.63 RM (133.30 S$)	+52%
Rent per month – apartment (1 bedroom) in city center	1,462.67 RM (494.06 S$)	8,556.22 RM (2,890.13 S$)	+485%
Price per square meter to buy apartment in city center	8,640.44 RM (2,918.58 S$)	72,143.95 RM (24,368.85 S$)	+735%

purported that if a visitor was spending $20 to see the attractions and eat at that 1939 World's Fair, by 2016 standards, they would have to spend about $340. The article gave the basic fair admission in 1939 at $0.75 while in 2016, it would be $12.76, but all the extra rides and other costs just like in Disneyland today added up to much more and the Minneapolis statisticians figured the $0.75 admission price in 1939 would rise to $20 if the extras were included. The inclusion of extras in 2016 would bring the total cost to $340.

According to the Federal Reserve Bank of St. Louis, the average hourly wage for "production and non-super-visory manufacturing" in 1939 was $0.50 while in 2016 it was $20.48. Assuming an 8-hour day, the daily wage average in 1939 would come to $4.00 and for 2016 it would be $163.84 per day. So, with the basic World's Fair admission at $0.75, it would take 18% of the average daily salary in 1939 but only 8% of the average daily salary in 2016. If visitors went the whole hog and took in all the major sights of the fair including the basic admission, the total at $20 would take five times their daily salary in 1939 but only two times their daily salary in 2016. It's a clear case of deflation and, more importantly, a World's Fair in 2016 with all the new visual and sound technology would be an entirely different experience than the one in 1939. My father and mother would be amazed at what they could see today and would also be pleased to see how much cheaper it would be.

Linking Income and Costs

It seems that all discussions of inflation have focused only on one part of the phenomenon: rising prices of goods and services. However, the actual impact such price rises have on people's lives has not been properly gauged. In order to do that it is necessary to compare the price rises with income rises. When that comparison is made, I find that in most cases average incomes have risen as fast or even faster than price rises. So, in human terms, I have had and are experiencing deflation. By linking the value of goods and services to the actual percentage of income required to purchase those goods and services, I can show that, in fact, we are in a deflating world, i.e. prices in relation to incomes are going down.

Deflation has led to positive outcomes for the world economy. As mentioned above, a good example of this is in food prices. Food prices, in fact, showed a huge fall between 1960 and 1980 and, despite a modest rise lasting until the late 1990s, have continued on this downward trend since then.

Deflation Statistics

Obtaining adequate data to compare the increases in products versus the increases in incomes is almost impossible since many data series do not contain the same product items and the years for which data is available for both goods and incomes do not match. It is therefore best to focus on food product categories since the characteristics of those items don't change substantially over time. For items such as automobiles, household appliances, and other manufactured items, clearly there has been a deflationary process taking place over the years because of dramatic changes in quality, efficiency, and utility. So, if I were to add those changes taking into account the quality and reliability improvements, the case for deflation would be enhanced.

I were able to obtain matching data for the US, Singapore, China, Japan, and India, but the yearly start and end dates differed between countries simply because of the lack of data. In any case, the admittedly sketchy statistics clearly point to global deflationary trends.

US Deflation

According to the US Bureau of Labor Statistics, between 1972 and 2017, households in the US increased their spending on shelter from 12% to 17%, increased that on pensions and insurance from 7% to 10%, and on healthcare from 5% to 7%, while spending on entertainment, apparel, food, and transportation went down. By 2017, the percent spent on apparel had gone down to about 3% of total household spending from about 12%. In other words, these essential items for survival – with the exception of shelter – had gone down and were gradually representing a smaller percentage of total expenditure. In the case of shelter, the numbers show that Americans enjoyed the largest average home size in the world so, on average, Americans had gone far beyond the basic shelter requirements.

Examining price changes in various food commodities and changes in average monthly wages received by regular employees in the US between 1930 and 2017, I found that wage increases far outpaced the increase in food prices. The basket of items included flour, poultry, beef, eggs, coffee, sugar, cheese, and milk. During the 1930 to 2017 period, prices changed from a low of 283% for eggs to a high of 1,571% for beef. At a compounded annual growth rate, the range was 8% for eggs and 18% for beef. For all products, the average growth was 13% annually. However, in studying the wage changes, monthly average wages went up from a low of 2,752% for the wholesale and retail trade workers to a high of 7,333% for agriculture, forestry, and fisheries workers. The compounded average annual growth rate ranged between 22% for the wholesale and retail trade workers, to a high of 28% for the agriculture, forestry, and fisheries workers. Overall, the average income increase for all workers between 1930 and 2017 was 3,538%. This, of course, is far in excess of the food price changes of 754%, a sure sign of deflation in real terms (Tables 8.2 and 8.3).

Table 8.2 US Percent Changes of Product Prices 1930 to 2017

Price Change	% CHANGE OF UNIT PRICE								% Change of average unit price of all food products
	Flour (per pound)	Poultry (per pound)	Beef (per pound)	Eggs (per dozen)	Coffee (per pound)	Sugar (per pound)	Cheese (per pound)	Milk (per quart)	
Price in 1930 (in USD)	0.05	0.37	0.34	0.52	0.40	0.06	0.59	0.14	
Price in 2017 (in USD)	0.47	1.90	5.68	1.99	4.29	0.63	4.03	0.73	
Unit Price % Change	840%	413%	1571%	283%	972%	950%	583%	421%	754%

Source: Data from US Bureau of Labor Statistics.[79]

Table 8.3 US Percent Changes of Average Monthly Wage Received by Regular Employees by Sector 1930 to 2017

Earning change	% Change of Monthly Earnings								
	Agriculture, forestry, fisheries	Manufacturing	Mining	Construction	Transportation	Communications and public utilities	Wholesale and retail trade	Finance insurance, real estate	% Change of average earnings of all sectors
Earning in 1930 (in USD)	388	1,488	1,424	1,526	1,610	1,499	1,569	1,973	
Earning in 2017 (in USD)	28,840	56,063	77,138	49,930	37,070	70,995	44,742	59,000	
Earnings % Change	7,333%	3,667%	5,317%	3,172%	2,202%	4,636%	2,752%	2,890%	3,996%

Source: Data from US Bureau of Labor Statistics.[79]

Singapore Deflation

Our investigations into changes in prices and incomes in Singapore covered the period between 2001 and 2017, the period for which reliable statistics could be obtained. I gathered prices for a wide range of 27 food items including such things as Thai rice, instant noodles, various fruits, sugar, instant coffee, etc. Then I looked at the median gross monthly income, including employer provident fund contributions of full-time employee residents including managers and administrators, work-ing proprietors, professionals, associate professionals and technicians, clerical support workers, service and sales workers, craftsmen and related trades workers, plant and machine operators and assemblers, and cleaners, laborers, and related workers. The average median gross monthly income between 2001 and 2017 increased by 52%.

During the same period, prices of various products rose by an average of slightly more than 52% as well (Tables 8.4 and 8.5). In essence, therefore, incomes in Singapore kept perfect pace with food price rises.

Japan Deflation

In Japan, I were able to obtain information from the Statistics Bureau of the Ministry of Internal Affairs and Communications, the Ministry of Health, Labour, and

Table 8.4 Singapore: Percent Changes of Product Prices in Singapore 2001 to 2017

Price Change	Thai rice (per 5 kg)	Bread (per 400 g)	Instant noodles (per 5 packets)	Pork (per 1 kg)	Beef (per 1k g)	Eggs (per 10 pcs)	Cooking oil (per 2 kg bottle)	Fish (per 1kg)	% Change of average unit price of all food products
Price in 2001 (in S$)	8.07	1.26	1.53	9.46	13.11	1.44	3.65	8.26	
Price in 2017 (in S$)	13.01	1.63	2.26	15.52	23.26	2.09	5.96	11.13	
Unit Price % Change	61%	29%	48%	64%	77%	45%	63%	35%	52%

Table 8.5 Singapore: Percent Changes of Average Monthly Wages Received by Regular Employees by Sector 2001 to 2017

Earnings Change	Managers & administrators	Working proprietors	Professionals	Associate professionals & technicians	Clerical support workers	Service & sales workers	Craftsmen & related trades workers	Plant & machine operators & assemblers	% Change of average earnings of all sectors
				% Change of Monthly Earnings					
Earnings in 2001 (in S$)	6,000	2,600	4,350	3,000	2,088	1,508	1,885	1,508	
Earnings in 2017 (in S$)	10,714	4,000	7,225	4,297	2,916	2,340	2,670	2,000	
Earnings % Change	79%	54%	66%	43%	40%	55%	42%	33%	52%

Welfare, and the Tokyo Statistical Yearbook for the period from 1963 to 2017.

Even though Japan experienced significant occupational change from the end of the mid-twentieth century, with the percentage of the labor force in agriculture decreasing from about 40% to less than 5%, food price increases were much lower than the changes in wages.

I focused on basic items such as white bread, wheat flour, tuna fish, beef, pork, tomatoes, apples, green tea, and sake. Notably – and unfortunately – the important item of rice was missing simply because control prices would have unnaturally depressed the overall average of price increases and would have inadvertently enhanced the deflation argument. Retail prices for key necessities such as salt and soy sauce remained unchanged since the early 1980s and, in some cases, 1980 retail prices for some items actually declined.

I looked at a range of occupations including clerks, typists, technicians, car drivers, general carpenters, general electricians, dentists, pharmacists, nurses, and professors of colleges and universities. For labor- or skill-intensive occupations, such as drivers, carpenters, etc., the average wage peaked around the 1990s, earlier than that of the knowledge-intensive occupations such as university professors and dentists. Then, wages for occupations after 2000 generally showed a slight downward trend.

Clearly, the average Japanese employee was not suffering from inflation of basic items. Looking at individual items in various occupations, taking one kilo of tuna fish, the percentage of monthly wages spent on consumption of tuna fish by technical workers between 1963 and 2017 went from 1.8% to 0.7%; for car drivers, it went from 1.4% to 0.7%; dentists from 0.9% to 0.4%; nurses from 2.3% to 0.8%. In the case of green tea, between 1963 and 2017, the percent of monthly wages spent on consumption of 1 kg of green tea, a very important part of the Japanese diet, for technical workers went from 2.1% to 1.2%; for car drivers from 1.7% to 1.3%; for dentists from 1.1% to 0.8%; for nurses from 2.7% to 1.5%, and so on. Overall, while food product prices between 1963 and 2017 rose by 405%, average monthly cash earnings rose by 1,030% – far more than the food prices. This was a clear indication of effective deflation in Japan (Tables 8.6 and 8.7).

India Deflation

Indian wage and commodity price numbers available between 1960 and 2010 showed that the percentage of wages spent on such items as rice, wheat, jowar (sorghum), bajra (millet), and maize actually went down for average salary workers. Rice, of course, is a staple in Indian diets. Jowar or sorghum is a staple, especially in

Table 8.6 Percent Changes of Product Prices 1963 to 2017

Price Change	White bread (1 kg)	Wheat flour (1 kg)	Tuna fish (1 kg)	Beef (1 kg)	Pork (1 kg)	Tomatoes (1 kg)	Apples (1 kg)	Green tea (1 kg)	Sake (1 L)	% Change of average price of all products
						Unit Price % Change				
Price in 1963	101.2	67.0	521.8	654.3	607.5	76.9	76.7	614.1	290.4	
Price in 2017	465.7	251.5	2,596.8	3,343.7	1,444.9	661.7	417.5	4,810.5	860.3	
Unit Price % Change	360%	275%	393%	411%	138%	760%	444%	683%	196%	405%

Table 8.7 Japan: Percentage Changes of Monthly Contractual Cash Earnings by Occupation 1963 to 2017

Earnings Change											
	% Changes of Monthly Contractual Cash Earnings										
	Clerks	Technicians	Car drivers	General carpenters	General electricians	Dentists	Pharmacists	Nurses	Professors of college and of university	% Change of average price of all products
Earnings in 1963	23,615	28,720	36,919	34,489	32,262	58,491	32,929	22,651	77,720	
Earnings in 2017	344,900	388,500	364,700	276,400	342,500	604,600	388,300	331,900	644,500	
Earnings % Change	1,361%	1,253%	888%	701%	962%	934%	1,079%	1,365%	729%	1,030%

the western and southern parts of the country where it is ground into flour and used to make rotis and other bread. Bajra or pearl millet is also widely used for bread and porridge.

The statistics show that for clerical and related workers, there were declines in how much of their income they spent on the commodities. In 1960, clerical and related workers spent about 0.4% of their monthly wages on rice while in 2010, it was down to 0.2%. Wheat went from 0.3% to 0.1%. Jowar fell from 0.3% to 0.1%. Bajra went from 0.3% to 0.1%. Maize for clerical and related workers fell from 0.2% of monthly salary in 1960 to 0.1% in 2010.

Even for farmers, fishermen, hunters, loggers, and related workers, the reduction in costs was evident. In that category of occupation, rice took 2.4% of their monthly salary in 1960 but only 0.3% in 2010. Wheat went from 1.8% to 0.2%, jowar from 1.5% to 0.1%, bajra from 1.6% to 0.2%, and maize from 1.2% of their monthly salary in 1960 to 0.2 in 2010.

If we look at non-food items, in 1960, teaching professionals would have had to spend 88 times or seven years of their monthly salary to purchase an automobile; but in 2010, it had come down to 33 times or about two and a half years. In 1960, a desktop computer would have cost a teacher about 4,441 times the salary; but by 2010 it had have come down to only 2 times.

A clerical worker in 1960 would require about 80 times his or her monthly salary to purchase a car; but by 2010, this had come down to 47 times. To buy a computer would have taken about 4,000 times a clerk's salary in 1960; but by 2010, it had come down to only 3 times.

For farmers, fishermen, and related workers in 1960, they would have had to send over 444 times their monthly salary to buy an automobile; but by 2010, it would take 69 times their monthly salary. Buying a desktop computer in 1960 would have taken 22,227 times or 1,852 years of their monthly salary; but by 2010, it was only 4 times – less than a half year.

In India, I were able to get historical wages prices between 1960 and 2010 from such sources as the Ministry of Statistics and the Labour Bureau of India. For average wages and salaries, I were able to obtain information for teaching professionals, clerical and related workers, farmers, fishermen, hunters, loggers, and related workers, salesman, shopping assistance and other sales workers, professional, technical and related workers, personal, and protective service workers.

India statistics show a dramatic example of deflation. Between 1960 and 2010, while product prices rose by 2,769%, average wages rose by 13,036% (Tables 8.8 and 8.9).

Table 8.8 India Percentage Change in Product Prices 1960 to 2010 (All India, Urban; Prices in Rs)

Price Change	Rice	Wheat	Jowar	Bajra	Maize	Total cereals	Automobile ambassador	Desktop computers	% Change of average price of all products
	(1 kg)	(1 kg)	(1 kg)	(1 kg)	(1 kg)	(1 kg)	(1 unit)	(1 unit)	
Price in 1960	0.63	0.48	0.41	0.43	0.33	0.54	12,000.0	600,000.0	
Price in 2010	19.38	15.20	11.81	11.81	12.38	17.19	498,000.0	30,000.0	
Unit Price % Change	2,976%	3,067%	2,778%	2,647%	3,651%	3,083%	4,050%	-95%	2,769%

Unit Price % Change

Table 8.9 India Percentage Changes of Average Monthly Wage/Salary Earnings Received by Regular Wage/Salaried Employees of Age 15–59 Years by Occupation Groups 1960 to 2010

Earnings (All India Urban-Earnings in INR)	% Changes of Monthly Earnings					% Change of average earnings of all occupations
	Teaching professionals	Clerical and related workers	Farmers, fishermen, hunters, loggers & related workers	Salesman, shopping Assistant and other sales workers	Personal and protective service workers	
Price in 1960	135.1	150.9	27.0	77.0	47.9	
Price in 2010	14,979.4	10,586.2	7,213.2	4,911.4	6,937.8	
Earning % Change	10,987%	6,915%	26,616%	6,278%	14,385%	13,036%

Sources: Ministry of Statistics and the Labour Bureau of India.[80]

China Deflation

I looked at wages and prices in China between 1995 and 2012 – the dates for which information was available. I were able to obtain information from the National Bureau of Statistics of China and the data source WIND. Products I were able to obtain information on included food grains, vegetables, meat, poultry eggs, aquatic products, sugar, alcoholic drinks, milk, and dairy products. During that period, price increases ranged between a low of 58% for eggs to a high of 443% for alcoholic drinks. This increase in the price of alcoholic drinks is probably attributable to the fact that with rising incomes in China, people were willing to pay more and go for more sophisticated and higher-priced products. If we look at the increase in prices for such iconic liquors as Kweichow Moutai, we can see how prices skyrocketed on the back of the popularity of that famous drink, which was a favorite for making toasts at the state dinners of Beijing luminaries such as Mao Tse Tung and Richard Nixon. Overall, the average increase in prices for all products came to 147% during the 1995 to 2012 period. But, indicating clear evidence of effective deflation during that same period, average wages rose by 755% (see (Tables 8.10 and 8.11).

Table 8.10 China: Percentage Changes of Product Prices 1995 to 2012

Price Change	Food grain	Vegetables	Meat	Poultry Eggs	Aquatic products	Alcoholic drinks	Milk and dairy products	% Change of average unit price of all food products
					% Change of Unit Price			
Price in 1995 (in RMB)	2.69	1.64	21.15	7.15	13.11	7.89	6.83	
Price in 2012 (in RMB)	5.82	4.47	37.30	11.31	26.92	42.82	10.97	
Unit Price % Change	116%	173%	76%	58%	105%	442%	61%	147%

Sources: National Bureau of Statistics of China and the data source WIND.[81]

Table 8.11 China: Percentage Changes of Average Monthly Wages Received by Regular Employees by Sector 1995 to 2012

Earnings Change	Public servants	Farmers, fishermen, hunters, loggers & related workers	Teaching professionals	Salesmen, shopping assistants, and other sales workers	Professional, scientific, and related workers	Personal and residential service workers	Miners, quarrymen, well drillers, and related workers	Manufacturing workers	% Change of average earnings of all sectors
				% Changes of Monthly Earnings					
Earnings in 1995 (in RMB)	460.5	293.5	452.9	354.0	570.5	498.5	479.8	430.8	
Earnings in 2012 (in RMB)	3,839.5	1,890.6	3,977.8	3,861.7	5,771.2	2,927.9	4,745.5	3,470.8	
Earnings % Change	732%	544%	778%	991%	912%	487%	889%	706%	755%

Sources: National Bureau of Statistics of China and the data source WIND.[81]

Bottom Line

Even if we accept that, while the measurement of inflation is in many cases faulty, we can see that prices have
indeed been rising over the last 50 years for some goods
that have seen few changes to their properties. But, as I
have tried to show, along with these rises in prices went
an increase in wages that, in most cases, was significantly
higher. So, even if you had to pay double the price for
eggs within a given period, if wages had doubled over the
same time you were not worse of than before. And what
is more, during that same period technological advances,
innovations and more effective production and distribution led to lower prices for many other goods. The result
of these developments is that we are actually living in a
deflationary world, one that improves our lives and is not
a sign of an economic slowdown but of an unprecedented level of innovation, automation and production
improvement.

9 Conclusions

Over the many years that mankind has attempted to measure the changing prices of goods and services, the results have left a lot to be desired. The complexity and remarkably changing environment have left statisticians and economists in a quandary over how to accurately measure changes in the prices of goods and services, and what they call "inflation." Nevertheless, numbers have been produced and, more importantly, those numbers have been used to make important policy decisions that impact millions of people. In the late 1990's and early 2000's those decisions were driven by the general consensus of economists that a little inflation, such as 2%, is a good thing, because it theoretically results in higher economic growth. They also theorized that excessive inflation is bad, because it impacts everyday lives and can result in political upheaval.

The inflation measures that serve as a basis for political decision-making, such as the Consumer Price Index (CPI), have been beset by enormous difficulties. Currencies with which the price indices are used suffer from continuous devaluation as governments debase their currencies, resulting in a loss of credibility among the population. The indices themselves are continuously changing in their composition as a result of statisticians' attempts to ensure they reflect changes in consumption. Of course, this means that an index from one period will be composed of different products/ services and weights than an index from another: it's like comparing apples and oranges. For these and other reasons I discussed in this book **inflation statistics cannot accurately reflect price changes in a reliable way**.

Another important phenomenon is the rise of deflation or the fall in prices of goods and services. There are a host of long-term developments which are driving an inexorable deflationary trend. Technological innovations impact all aspects of our lives, from robotics to gene therapy. The improvement of information flows means that we are receiving and handling information at a speed and quantity never before seen in the history of humanity, with artificial intelligence manufacturing being transformed, as well as food production and distribution. Each year, over 1.5 billion smartphones are sold: They are becoming ubiquitous in even the remotest places in the world. The power of those smartphones far surpasses the largest computers developed 20 years ago. It might be said that mankind is now experiencing Moore's Law as society benefits exponentially as a result of productivity increases.

These unprecedented levels of innovation, automation and globalisation have been driving down prices and improving the quality of many goods and services.

In such an environment in a commodity money system where there is a limited amount of currency, there would be falling prices and deflation; but, with the elastic and increasing supply of our paper money systems inflation numbers have been rising, and in some cases have rocketed into hyperinflation. The predictability of price levels has decreased since, with the fractional-reserve system, there is no incentive to produce the exact amount of money that would keep prices stable.

However, **inflation numbers have not been growing in isolation. Wages and incomes have been rising as well and in many cases at a faster pace**. Workers on average today require fewer hours to be able to afford a new refrigerator or TV set than a worker 20 or 50 years ago, and today they would also get a more advanced product. **Relative to incomes many prices for products and services have not risen but in fact have declined and continue to decline**.

The net effect of the above mentioned developments is that instead of inflation, we have been experiencing deflation. People are better off now than they were in the past. They will continue to improve their lives as innovation and automation drive productivity and lower prices and their incomes outpace the cost of things they need to buy and services they need to access. This deflationary phenomenon is here to stay and will continue to improve our standard of living for the foreseeable future.

Welcome to the wonderful world of deflation!

REFERENCES

1 (2012). *United Nations General Assembly, 67th Session, 7th Plenary Meeting*. New York: United Nations. Retrieved from https://undocs.org/en/A/67/PV.7.

2 Hayek, F. A. (1976). *The Denationalization of Money*. London: The Institute of Economic Affairs.

3 *September/October 1978 Campaign Speech Draft*. (n.d.). Retrieved from Ronald Reagan Presidential Library Digital Library Collections: https://www.reaganlibrary .gov/sites/default/files/digitallibrary/1980campaign/ box-024/40-656-7386263-024-001-2017.pdf.

4 *House of Commons Hansard Debates*. (1991, May 16). Retrieved fromwww.parliament.uk: https://publications .parliament.uk/pa/cm199091/cmhansrd/1991-05-16/ Orals-1.html.

5 Polo, M., & da Pisa, R. (1300). *The Travels of Marco Polo*.

6 *FOMC Statement*. (2008, September 16). Retrieved from Federal Reserve Board: https://www.federalreserve.gov/ newsevents/pressreleases/monetary20080916a.htm.

7 Summer, S. (2015). "In Retrospect, That Decision Was Certainly a Mistake." The Library of Economics and Liberty. Retrieved from https://www.econlib.org/ archives/2015/10/in_retrospect_t.html.

8 Morrison, R. (2013, July 31). *Remembering Milton Friedman*. Retrieved from https://taxfoundation.org/ remembering-milton-friedman/.

9   Keynes, J. M. (1920). *The Economic Consequences of the Peace.* London: Macmillan and Co., Limited. Retrieved from https://archive.org/stream/economicconseque00key nuoft?ref=ol#page/220/mode/2up/ search/By+a+continui ng+process+of+inflation.

10 Sowell, T. (2012, December 4). *Fiscal Cliff Notes.* Retrieved from Creators: https://www.creators.com/read/ thomas-sowell/12/12/fiscal-cliff-notes.

11 Rand, A. (1962, May). "Who Will Protect Us from Our Protectors?" *The Objectivist Newsletter.*

12 Hemingway, E. (1935, September). "Notes on the Next War: A Serious Topical Letter." *Esquire Magazine,* IV(iii). Retrieved from http://archive.esquire.com/article/1935/ 9/1/notes-on-the-next-war.

13 Hoover, H. (1935, October 5). *Spending, Deficits, Debts, and Their Consequences.* Oakland, California, United States of America. Retrieved from https://hoover.archives .gov/sites/default/files/research/ebooks/ b3v1_full.pdf.

14 Indrawati, S. M. (2011, April 28). "Ex-protest Leader Mulyani Shakes Up World Bank." (A. Brummer, Interviewer) ThisisMoney.co.uk. Retrieved from https:// www.thisismoney.co.uk/money/news/ article-1721523/ Ex-protest-leader-Mulyani-shakes-up-World-Bank.html.

15 Callaghan, J. (1976, September 28). *Labour Party Annual Conference.* Blackpool. Retrieved from http://www.british politicalspeech.org/speech-archive.htm?speech=174.

16 Deming, W. E. (1980, September 8). "'Made in Japan' Is No Joke Now, Thanks to Edwards Deming: His New Problem Is 'Made in U.S.A.'" (C. Crawford-Mason,

Interviewer) People.com. Retrieved from https://people .com/archive/made-in-japan-is-no-joke-now-thanks-to- edwards-deming-his-new-problem- is-made-in-u-s-a-vol- 14-no-10/.

17 Yellen, J. (2014, July 2). *Monetary Policy and Financial Stability*. Washington, DC, United States of America. Retrieved from https://www.federalreserve.gov/new sevents/speech/yellen20140702a.htm.

18 Bowles, C. (1946, February 18). *Congressional Committee*. United States of America.

19 Rajan, R. (2014, August 5). India Central Bank. Retrieved from http://time.com/3099587/india-central- bank-raghuram-rajan-global-finance-world-economy/.

20 Friedman, M., & Friedman, R. (1980). *Free to Choose: A Personal Statement*. New York: Harcourt Brace Jovanovich, Inc. Retrieved from http://www.proglocode.unam.mx/ sites/proglocode.unam.mx/files/docencia/Milton%20 y%20Rose%20Friedman%20-%20Free%20to%20 Choose.pdf.

21 Mises, L. v. (1944). *Omnipotent Government: The Rise of the Total State and Total War*. Yale University Press. Retrieved from https://mises.org/sites/default/files/ Omnipotent Government The Rise of the Total State and Total War_3.pdf.

22 Mises, L. v. (1990). *Economic Freedom and Interventionism: An Anthology of Articles and Essays*. Retrieved from https://mises.org/library/economic- freedom-and-interventionism/html/p/123.

23 Beta, T. (2011). *Master of Stupidity*. Self-published.

24 Hazlitt, H. (1946). *Economics in One Lesson*. Harper & Brothers. Retrieved from https://www.liberalstudies.ca/wp-content/uploads/2014/11/Economics-in-One-Lesson_2.pdf.

25 Brady, K. (2013, June 4). *OP-ED: Fix growth gap, create prosperity*. Retrieved from United States Congress Joint Economic Committee: https://www.jec.senate.gov/public/index.cfm/republicans/2013/6/fix-growth-gap-create-prosperity.

26 Premji, A. (2011, October 21). "Charlie Rose Talks to Wipro's Azim Premji." (C. Rose, Interviewer) Bloomberg Businessweek. Retrieved from https://www.bloomberg.com/news/articles/2011-10-20/charlie-rose-talks-to-wipro-s-azim-premji

27 Samuelson, P. (1958). *What is the most important economic problem to be faced by the United States in the next twenty years?* Committee for Economic Development. Retrieved from https://www.nobelprize.org/prizes/economic-sciences/1970/samuelson/biographical/

28 Feldstein, M. (2006). Panel Discussion: Central Banking: Is Science Replacing Art? *Monetary policy: a journey from theory to practice – an ECB colloquium held in honour of Otmar Issing*. Frankfurt am Main: European Central Bank. Retrieved from https://www.ecb.europa.eu/pub/pdf/other/monetarypolicyjourneytheorypractice2007en.pdf?955e0a69a7c01a3265ab8b19deb448f2.

29 Kiyosaki, R. (2007, March 5). "Rich Today, Poor Tomorrow." Retrieved from Rich Dad Company: https://

www.richdad.com/resources/articles/rich-today-poor-
tomorrow.

30 *Inflation.* Retrieved from Investoquotia: http://
investoquotia.com/amnesomrade/inflation/.

31 Chang, H.-j. (2007). *Bad Samaritans: The Myth of Free
Trade and the Secret History of Capitalism.* Bloomsbury
Press. Retrieved from http://investoquotia.com/
amnesomrade/inflation/.

32 Powell, J. (2016, November 29). *Recent Economic
Developments and Longer-Run Challenges.* Indianapolis,
Indiana, United States of America. Retrieved from https://
www.federalreserve.gov/newsevents/speech/files/powell
20161129a.pdf

33 Yellen, J. (1995). *Meeting of the Federal Open Market
Committee.* Washington, DC: The Federal Reserve
System. Retrieved from https://www.federalreserve.gov/
monetarypolicy/files/FOMC19950201meeting.pdf.

34 Bernanke, B. (2009, November 2). *Downside Danger.*
Retrieved from ForeignPolicy.com: https://foreignpolicy
.com/2009/11/02/downside-danger.

35 Bernanke, B. (2002, November 21). "Deflation: Making
Sure 'It' Doesn't Happen Here." Washington, DC, United
States of America: The Federal Reserve Board. Retrieved
from https://www.federalreserve.gov/boarddocs/speeches/
2002/20021121

36 Friedman, M. (1970). *The Counter-Revolution in
Monetary Theory.* London: Institute of Economic Affairs.
Retrieved from https://miltonfriedman.hoover.org/
friedman_images/Collections/2016c21/IEA_1970.pdf.

37 Kiyosaki, R. (2007, February 16). "Throwing Good Money After Bad." Retrieved from Rich Dad Company: https://www.richdad.com/resources/articles/throwing-good-money-after-bad.

38 Surowiecki, J. (2009, September 7). "Inflated Fears." Retrieved from The New Yorker: https://www.newyorker.com/magazine/2009/09/14/inflated-fears

39 Powell, J. (2011, November 29). "Rich Nations that Went Broke by Spending Too Much." Retrieved from Forbes: https://www.forbes.com/sites/jimpowell/2011/11/29/rich-nations-that-went-broke-by-spending-too-much/.

40 Surowiecki, J. (2009, June 8). "Change We Can't Believe In." Retrieved from The New Yorker: https://www.newyorker.com/magazine/2009/06/08/change-we-cant-believe-in.

41 Bhattacharya, A. (2017, June 15). "Indian Banks' Exposure to Telecom 'Not that Huge'". Arundhati Bhattacharya, SBI (E. Now, Interviewer) *Economic Times*. Retrieved from https://economictimes. indiatimes.com/markets/expert-view/indian-banks-exposure-to-telecom-not-that-huge-arundhati- bhattacharya-chairman-sbi/articleshow/59138650.cms.

42 Gross, B. (2012, November 19). "Wisdom from the Bond King." (M. Morella, Interviewer) U.S. News & World Report. Retrieved from https://money.usnews.com/money/personal-finance/mutual-funds/ articles/2012/11/19/bill-gross-how-investors-can-navigate-the-new-normal.

43 Vickrey, W. (1986, September). "Budget-Smudget. Why
    Balance What, How, and When?" Atlantic *Economic
    Journal*, 14(3). Retrieved from https://doi.org/10.1007/
    BF02304618.

44 Oberhelman, D. R. (2013, May 17). "Caterpillar's Doug
    Oberhelman: Manufacturing's Mouthpiece." (M. Kimes,
    Interviewer) Bloomberg Businessweek. Retrieved from
    https://www.bloomberg.com/news/articles/2013-05-16/
    caterpillars-doug-oberhelman-manufacturings-mouthpiece.

45 Wriston, W. B. (1986). *Risk and Other Four-Letter Words*.
    New York: Harper & Row.

46 Mises, L. v. (1974). *Planning for Freedom and Twelve
    Other Essays and Addresses*. Libertarian Press. Retrieved
    from https://mises-media.s3.amazonaws.com/
    Planning%20for%20Freedom%20and%20 Twelve%20
    other%20Essays%20and%20Addresses_2.pdf.

47 Grassley, C. (2009, August 25). "Senator Warns of
    Hyperinflation Rivaling the 1980s." (M. O'Brien,
    Interviewer) The Hill. Retrieved from https://thehill
    .com/blogs/blog-briefing-room/news/lawmaker-news/
    56137-senator-warns-of-hyperinflation-rivaling-the-
    1980s.

48 Sowell, T. (2012, December 10). "Sometimes
    Government's Biggest Tax Bite Is Out Of Poor." Retrieved
    from Investor's Business Daily: https://www.investors
    .com/politics/commentary/governments-steal-through-
    inflation/

49 Geithner, T. (2009, March 29). "This Week with George
    Stephanopoulos." (G. Stephanopoulos, Interviewer)

50 Kotlikoff, L. (2006). "Is the United States Bankrupt?"
    Federal Reserve Bank of St. Louis Review, 235–49.
    Retrieved from https://files.stlouisfed.org/files/htdocs/
    publications/review/06/07/Kotlikoff.pdf.

51 Hazlitt, H. (1960). *What You Should Know About
    Inflation*. New York: D. Van Nostrand Company, Inc.
    Retrieved from https://mises-media.s3.amazonaws.com/
    What%20You%20Should%20Know%20About%20
    Inflation_3.pdf.

52 Rockwell, L. H. (2008, December 2). "The Force is with
    Us." Retrieved from LewRockwell.com: https://www
    .lewrockwell.com/2008/12/lew-rockwell/the-force-is-
    with-us/.

53 Schiff, P. (2013, August 20). "The GDP Distractor."
    Retrieved from Business Insider: https://www.business
    insider.com/the-gdp-distractor-2014-2.

54 Johnson, P. (2015). *UK Consumer Price Statistics: A
    Review*. UK Statistics Authority.

55 Kennedy, R. F. (1968). "Remarks at the University of
    Kansas." JFK Library. Retrieved from https://www
    .jfklibrary.org/learn/about-jfk/the-kennedy-family/
    robert-f-kennedy/robert-f-kennedy-speeches/
    remarks-at-the-university-of-kansas-march-18-1968.

56 Baker, D. (2014, September 26). "That Two Percent
    Inflation Target and Silly Things Economists Say."
    Retrieved from Beat the Press, Center for Economic and
    Policy Research: http://cepr.net/blogs/beat-the-press/
    that-two-percent-inflation-target-and-silly-things-
    economists-say.

57 Stockman, D. (2015, December 18). "Sell The Bonds, Sell The Stocks, Sell The House, Dread The Fed!" Retrieved from David Stockman's Contra Corner: https://davidstockmanscontracorner.com/sell-the-bonds-sell-the-stocks-sell-the-house-dread-the-fed/.

58 Brainard, L. (2018). *Sustaining Full Employment and Inflation around Target.* New York: Federal Reserve Board. Retrieved from https://www.federalreserve.gov/news events/speech/brainard20180531a.htm.

59 Powell, J. H. (2018). *Semiannual Monetary Policy Report to the Congress.* Washington DC: Bank for International Settlements. Retrieved from https://www.bis.org/review/r180307e.pdf.

60 Bevacqua, G. (2012, December). "A Life in Statistics." (A. Carriquiry, Interviewer) Significance. Retrieved from https://rss.onlinelibrary.wiley.com/doi/pdf/10.1111/j.1740-9713.2012.00621.x.

61 "US Media Sets Eyes on Argentina's 'Manipulation of Numbers'." (2009, August 18). Retrieved from MercoPress: https://en.mercopress.com/2009/08/18/us-media-sets-eyes-on-argentinas-manipulation-of-numbers.

62 "Is China Faking its Economic Growth?" (2012, February 16). Retrieved from CNNMoney: https://money.cnn.com/2012/02/16/news/economy/china_chanos/index.htm.

63 Fukui, T. (2004, July 5). Opening Speech by Toshihiko Fukui, Governor of the Bank of Japan, at the 11th International Conference sponsored by the Institute for

Monetary and Economic Studies. Japan: Bank of Japan. Retrieved from https://www.boj.or.jp/en/announcements/press/koen_2004/ko0407a.htm/.

64 Hudson, M. (2016, April 6). "The Slow Crash." *Guns and Butter podcast.* (B. Faulkner, Interviewer) Retrieved from http://gunsandbutter.org/transcript-the-slow-crash.

65 Moelis, K. (2016, October 12). "Wall Street's Star Dealmaker Ken Moelis on What's Driving Today's M&A, Hiring Millennials, and What He Really Meant to Say about Donald Trump." (M. Turner, Interviewer) Business Insider. Retrieved from https://www.businessinsider.com/ken-moelis-bi-interview-2016-10.

66 Grant, J. (2014, October 5). "Jim Grant: We're in an Era of Central Bank Worship." (H. Bonner, Interviewer) ZeroHedge. Retrieved from https://www.zerohedge.com/news/2014-10-05/jim-grant-we%E2%80%99re-era-central-bank-worship.

67 Shedlock, M. (2009, April 16). "Deflation Has Gone Global." Retrieved from MISH'S Global Economic Trend Analysis: http://globaleconomicanalysis.blogspot.com/2009/04/deflation-has-gone-global.html.

68 Rothbard, M. N. (1991, April). "Deflation, Free or Compulsory." *The Free Market*, 9(4). Retrieved from https://mises.org/library/deflation-free-or-compulsory.

69 Cresswell, P. (2014, November 21). "Quotes of the Day: On Deflation." Retrieved from Not PC: http://pc.blogspot.com/2014/11/quotes-of-day-on-deflation.html.

70 Reisman, G. (2003, August 18). "The Anatomy of Deflation." Retrieved from Mises Institute: *https://mises .org/library/anatomy-deflation.*

71 Ghosn, C. (2002, December 16). "Q&A: Carlos Ghosn: What Japan Needs Is a Vision." Bloomberg Businessweek. Retrieved from https://www.bloomberg.com/news/ articles/2002-12-15/q-and-a-carlos-ghosn-what-japan-needs-is-a-vision.

72 World Economic Forum. (2015, February 4). "Davos 2015 - Ending the Experiment" [Video file]. Retrieved from https://www.youtube.com/watch?v=fIa8sN2lPUs.

73 Dowd, M. (1987, June 28). "Is Jack Kemp Mr. Right?" *The Times.* Retrieved from https://www.nytimes.com/ 1987/06/28/magazine/is-jack-kemp-mr-right.html.

74 Davies, G. (2008, November 13). "We Must Start Thinking Like South American Dictators." Retrieved from *The Guardian*: https://www.theguardian.com/ commentisfree/2008/nov/13/economy-inflation-deflation-bank-england.

75 Shedlock, M. (2009, November 2). "Is Debt-Deflation Just Beginning?" Retrieved from MISH'S Global Economic Trend Analysis: http://globaleconomicanalysis .blogspot.com/2009/11/is-debt-deflation-just-beginning .html.

76 (n.d.). Retrieved from Kleiner Perkins: https://www .kleinerperkins.com/.

77 (n.d.). Retrieved from Airbnb: https://www.airbnb.com/.

78 (n.d.). Retrieved from Uber: https://www.uber.com/.

79 (n.d.). Retrieved from U.S. Bureau of Labor Statistics:
    https://www.bls.gov/.

80 (n.d.). Retrieved from Ministry of Statistics and
    Programme Implementation, Government of India:
    http://www.mospi.gov.in/.

81 (n.d.). Retrieved from National Bureau of Statistics of
    China: http://www.stats.gov.cn/.

INDEX